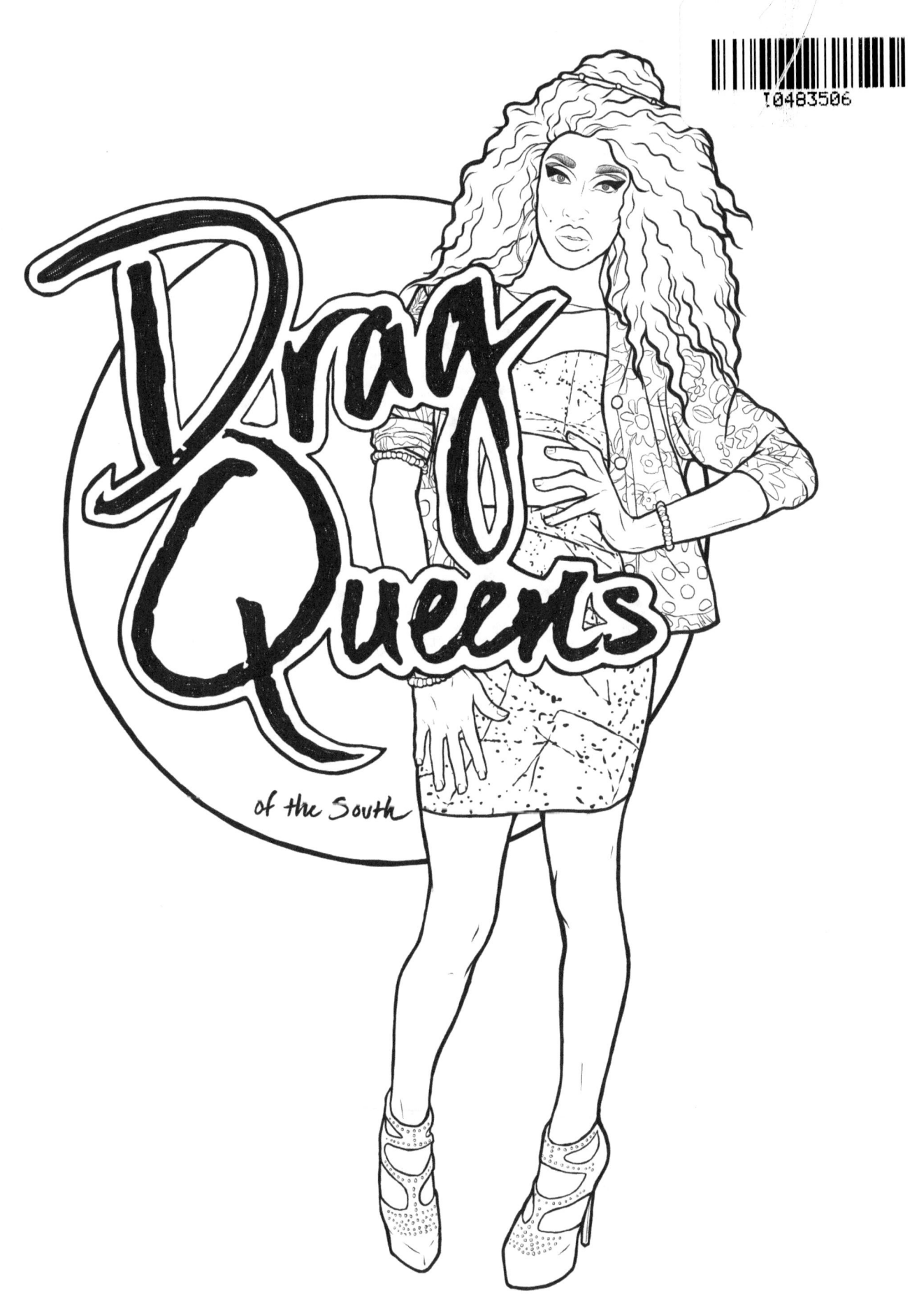

Drag Queens
of the South

A COLORING BOOK • BY KASTEN McCLELLAN SEARLES

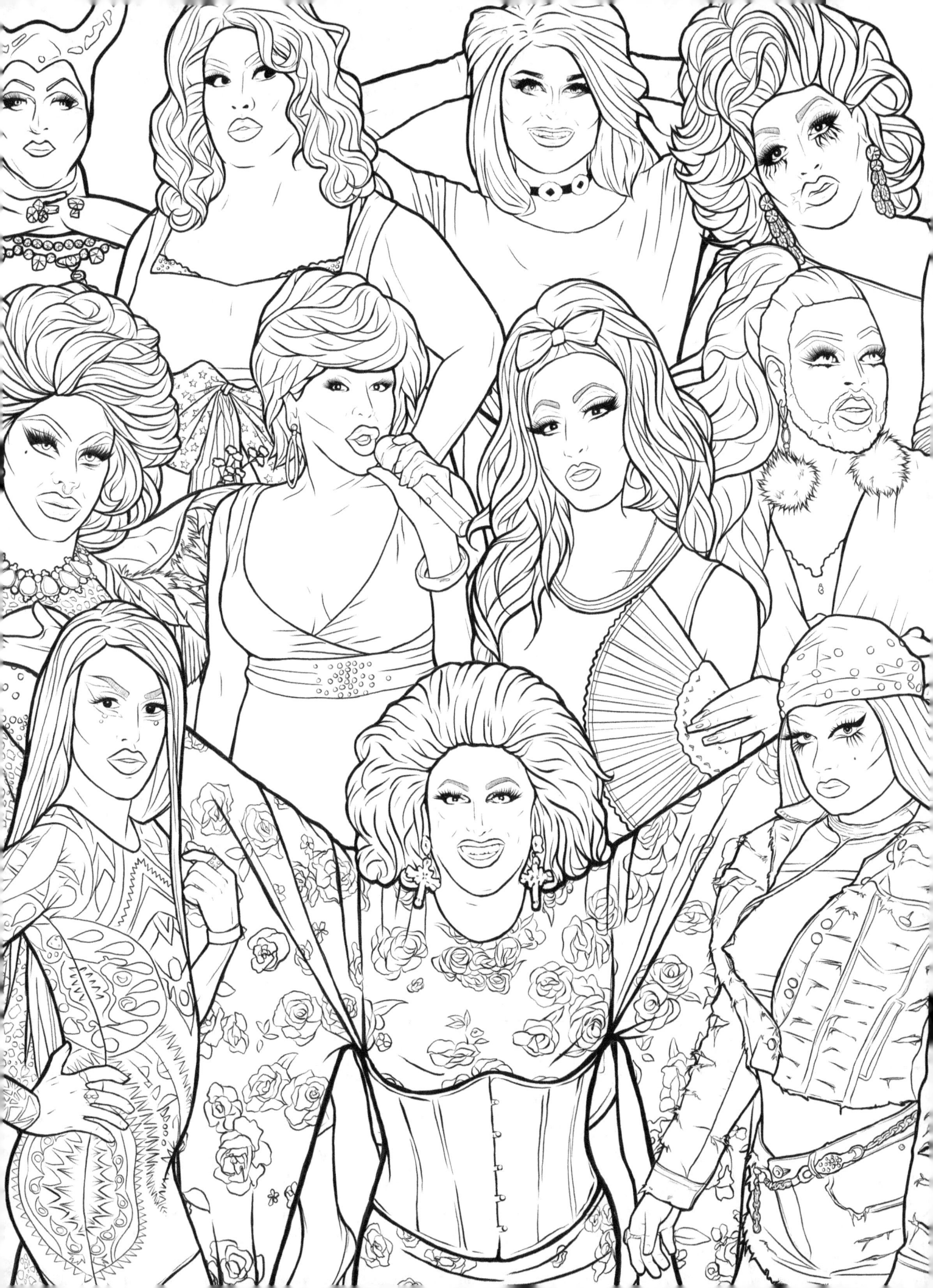

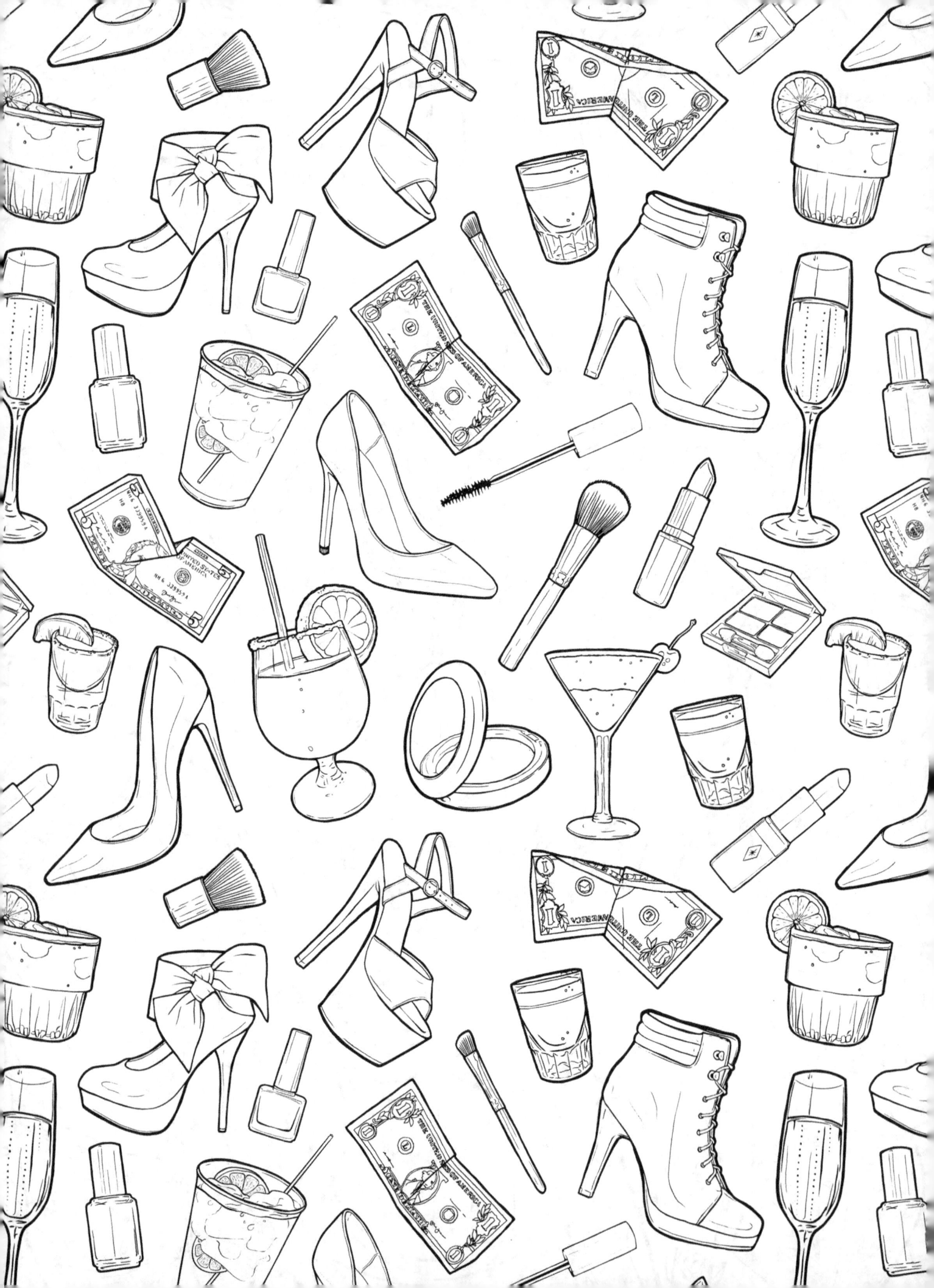

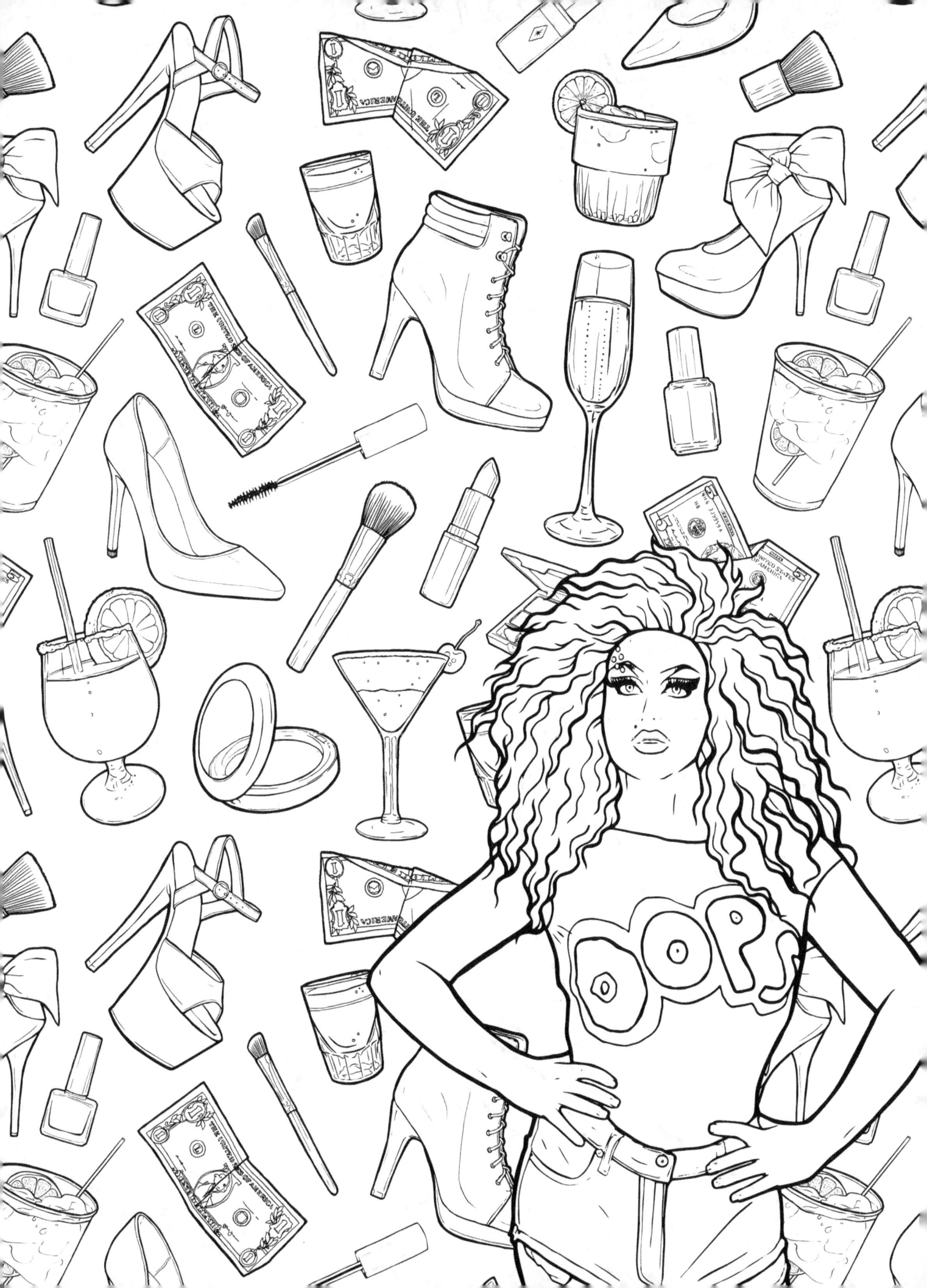

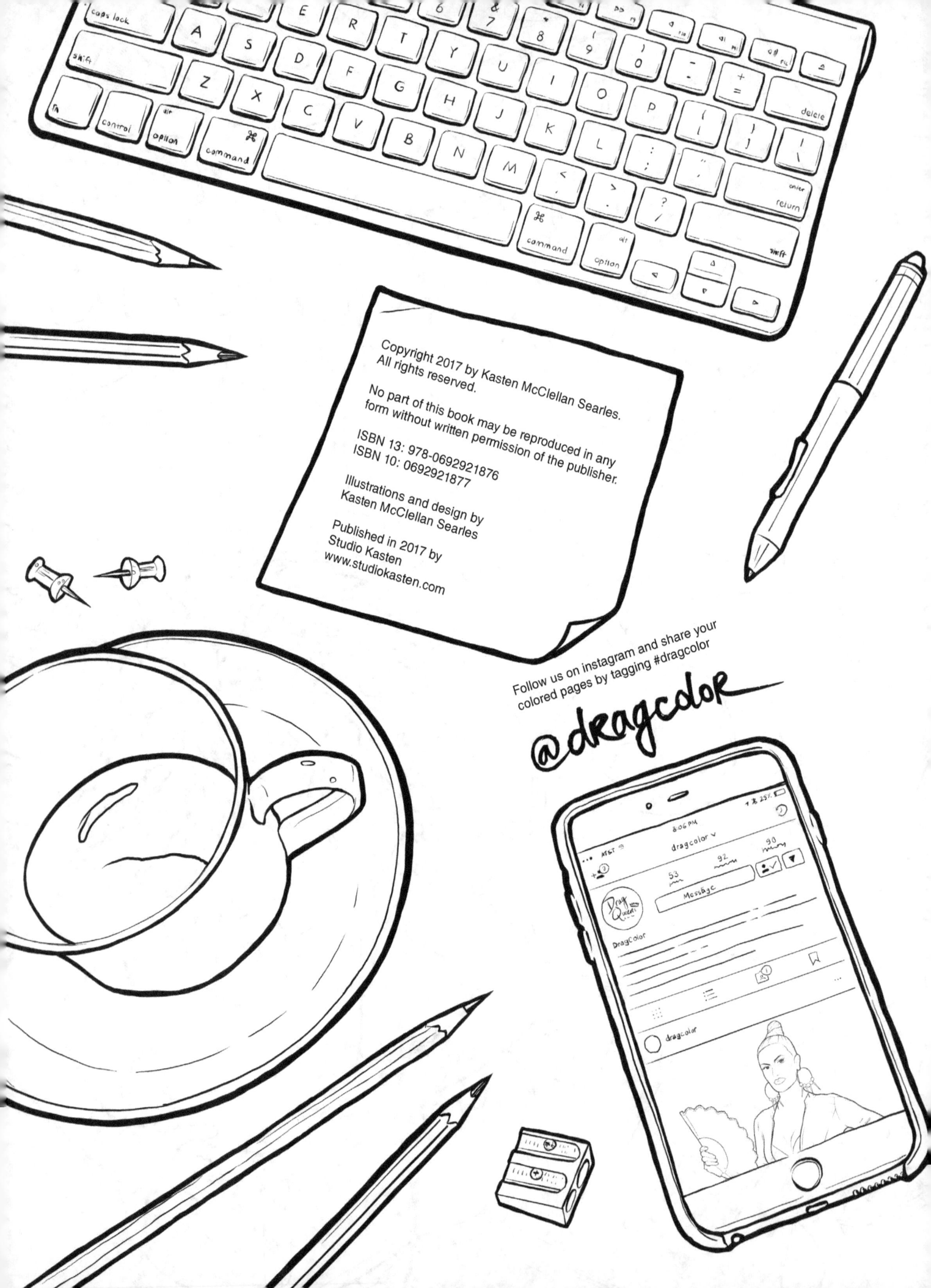

Illustrations and design by
Kasten McClellan Searles

Published in 2017 by
Studio Kasten
www.studiokasten.com

Follow us on instagram and share your
colored pages by tagging #dragcolor

@dragcoloR

This coloring book is dedicated to the drag performers
and backers that helped make it possible. Thank you for
helping make this project a reality!

Each illustration highlights a real drag king or queen that
calls the South home. We can't wait to see how you color
these talented performers. Please share your work with
the tag #dragcolor. The pages are printed on one side only
to ensure that any bleed through will not harm the next
illustration. I suggest coloring with sharp colored pencils.
If you like to color with markers test them for bleed through
and use a blank sheet of paper underneath to protect the
next spread.

Have fun coloring and
SUPPORT YOUR LOCAL DRAG QUEENS!
Kasten McClellan Searles

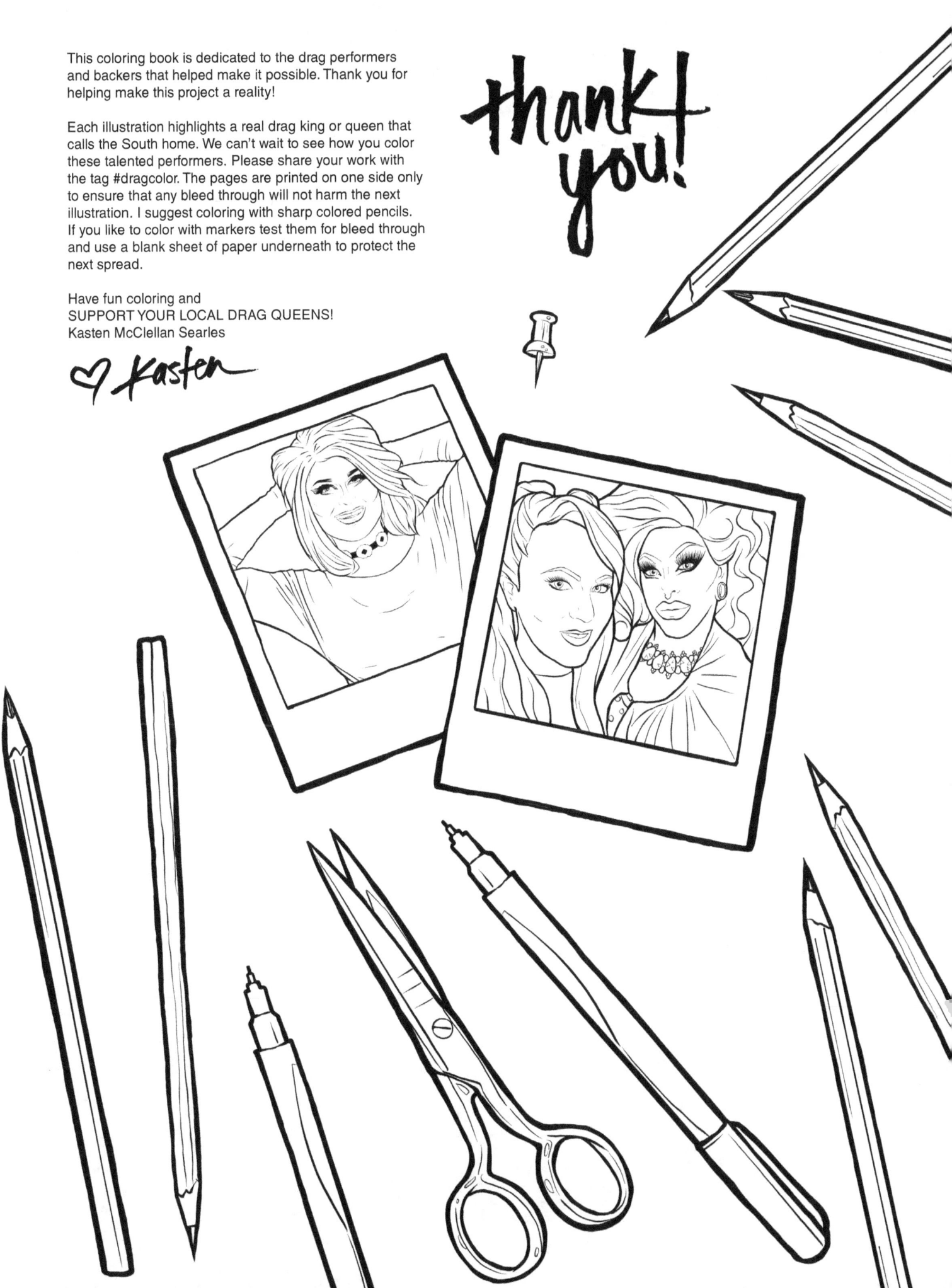

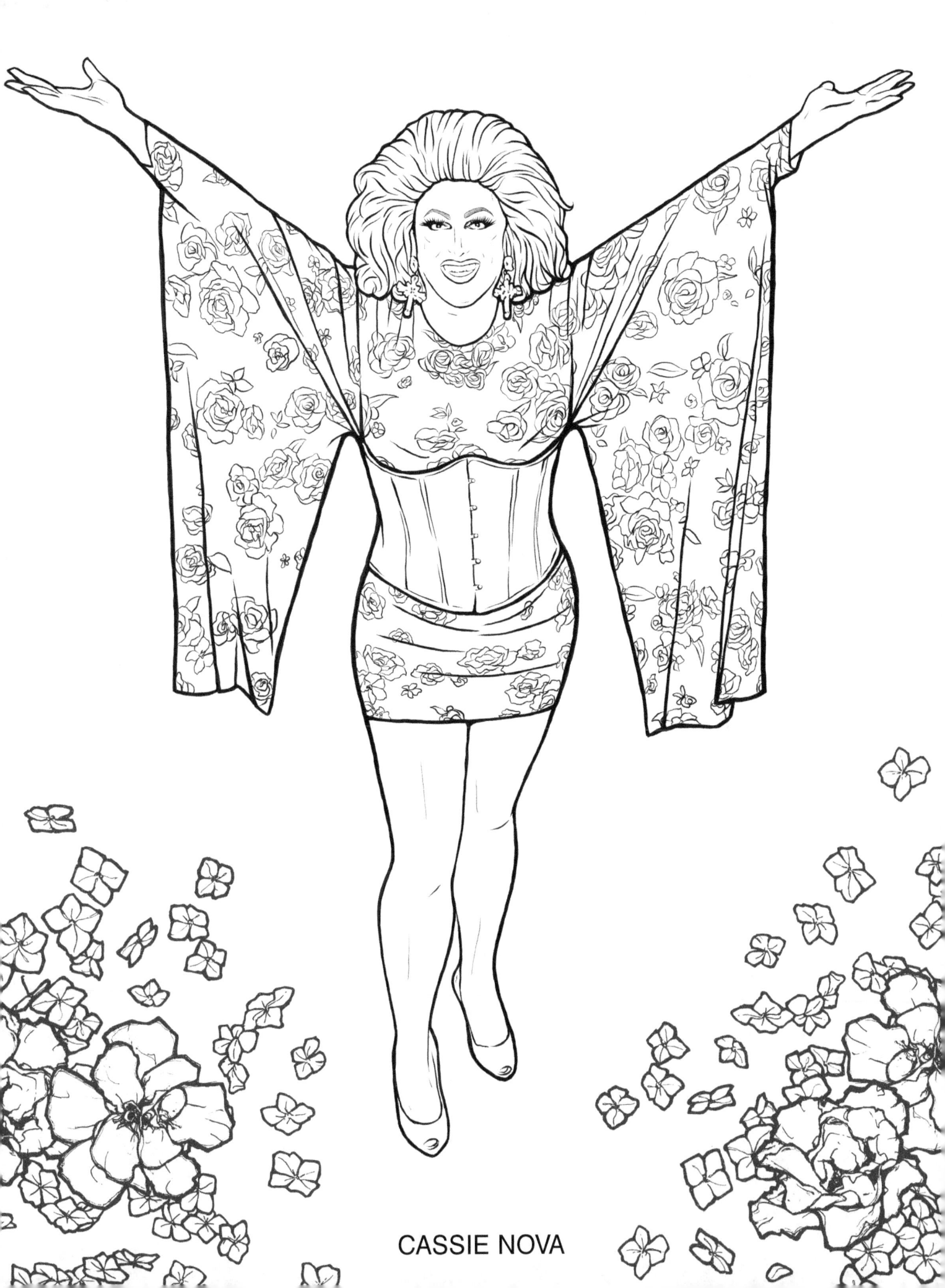

CASSIE NOVA

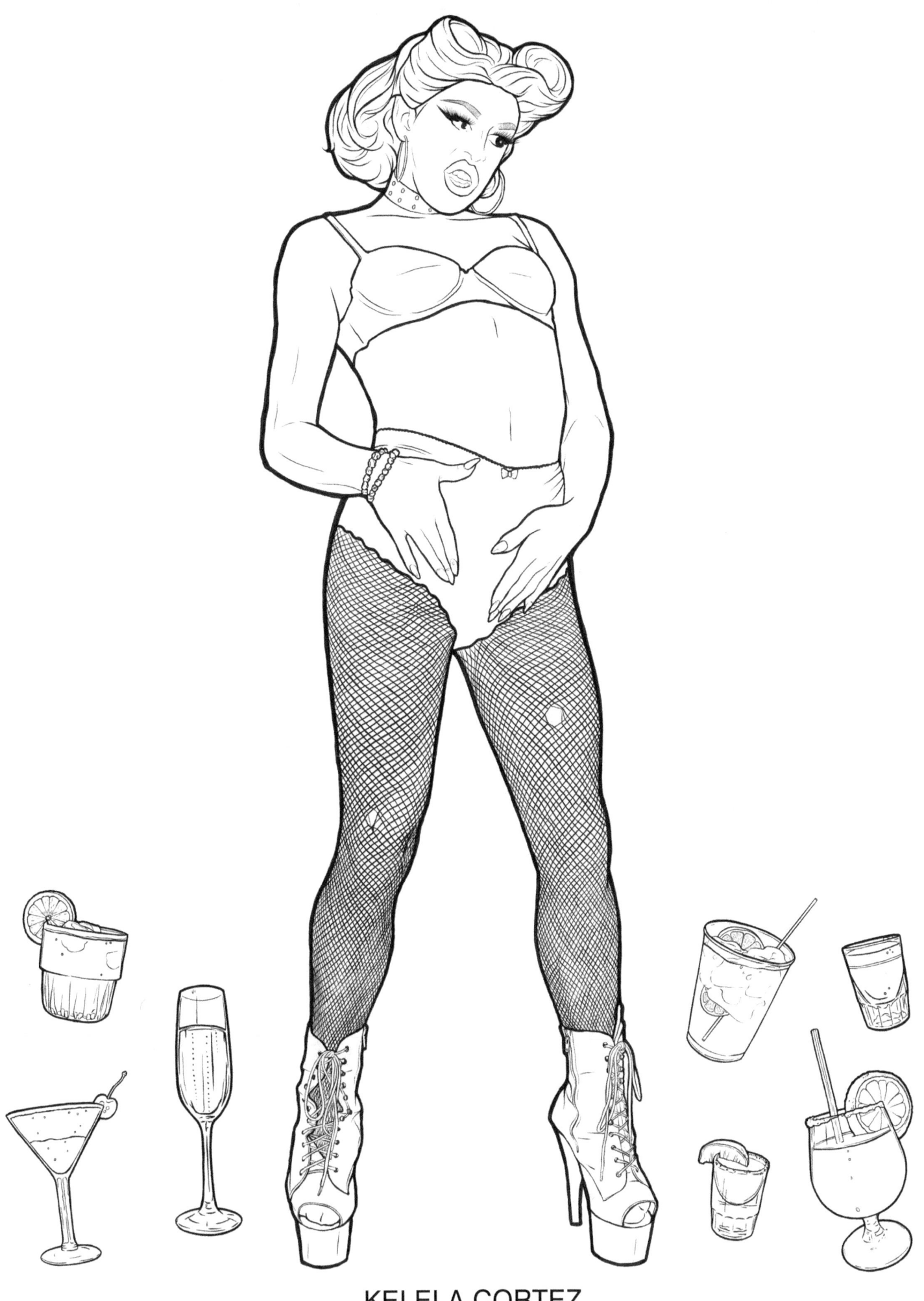

KELELA CORTEZ

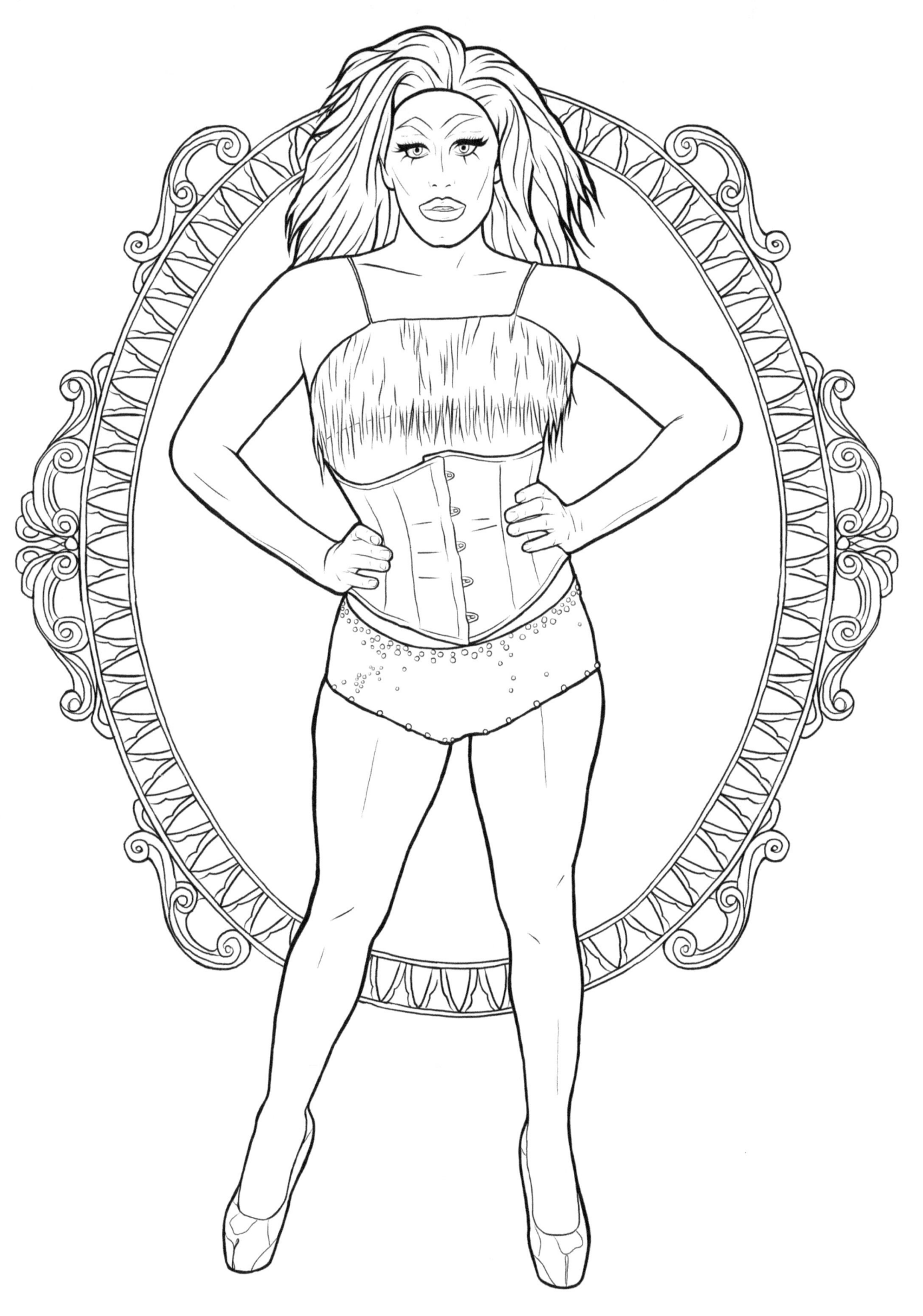

PRISCILLA ROCK

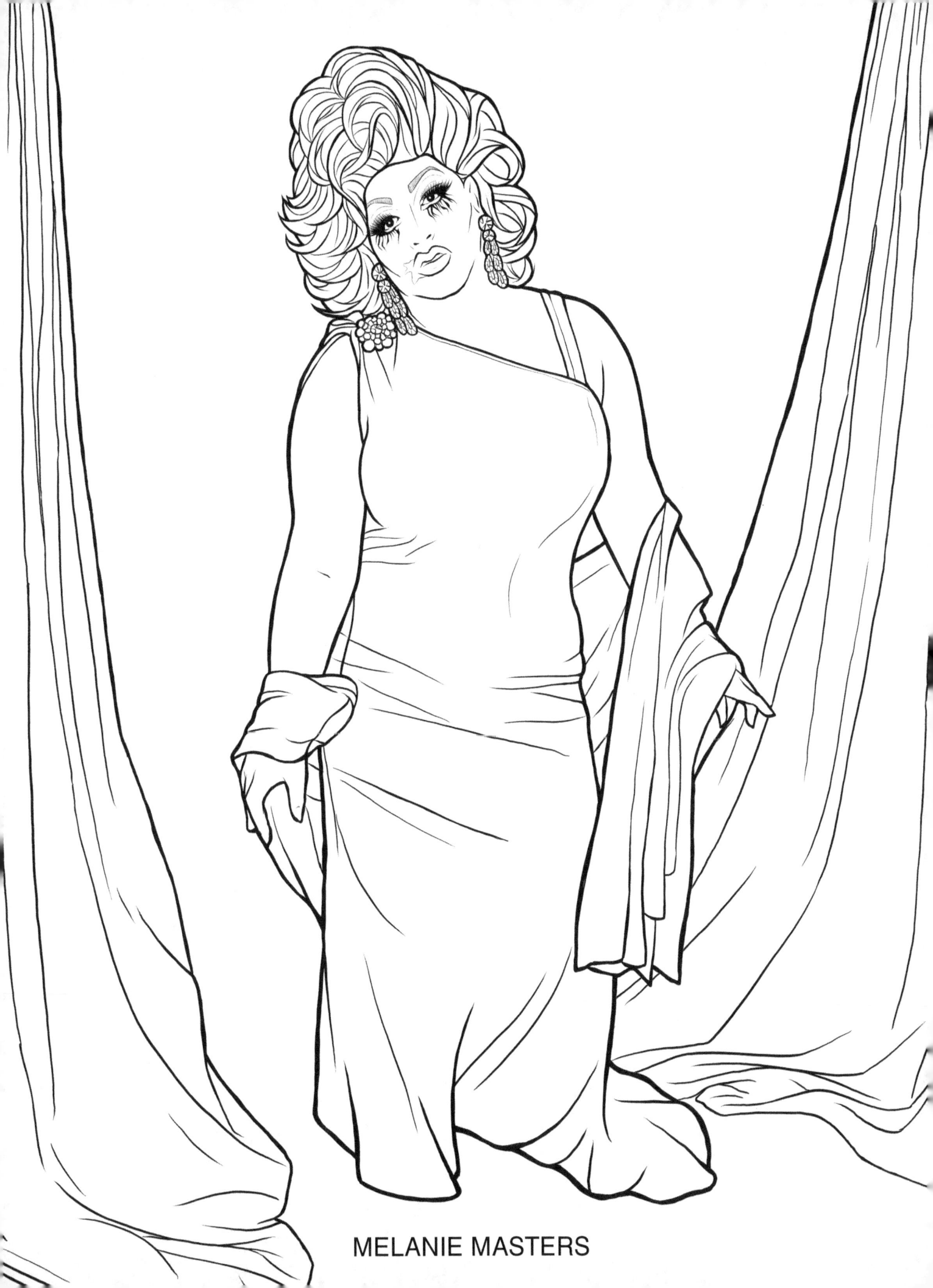

MELANIE MASTERS

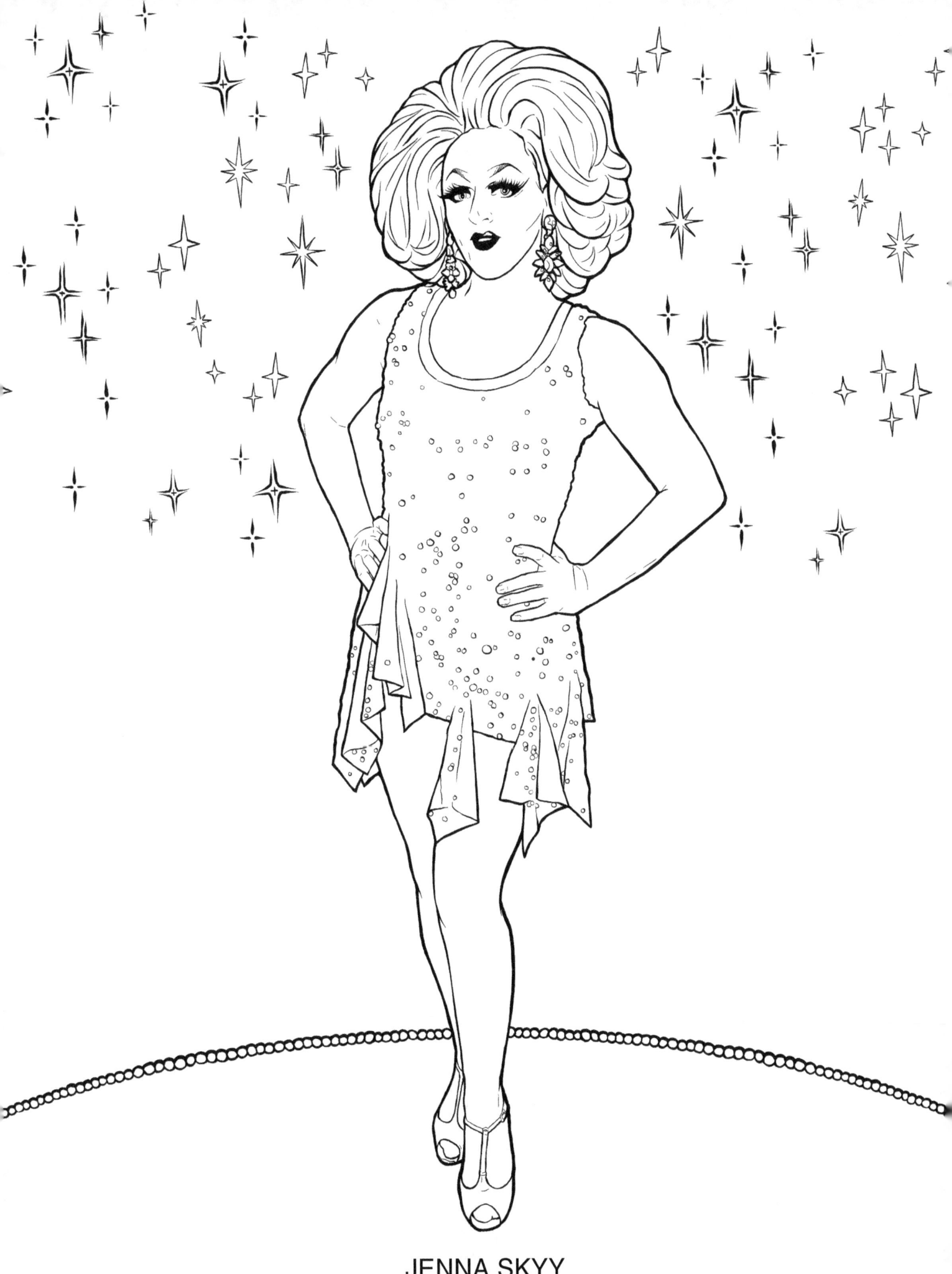

JENNA SKYY

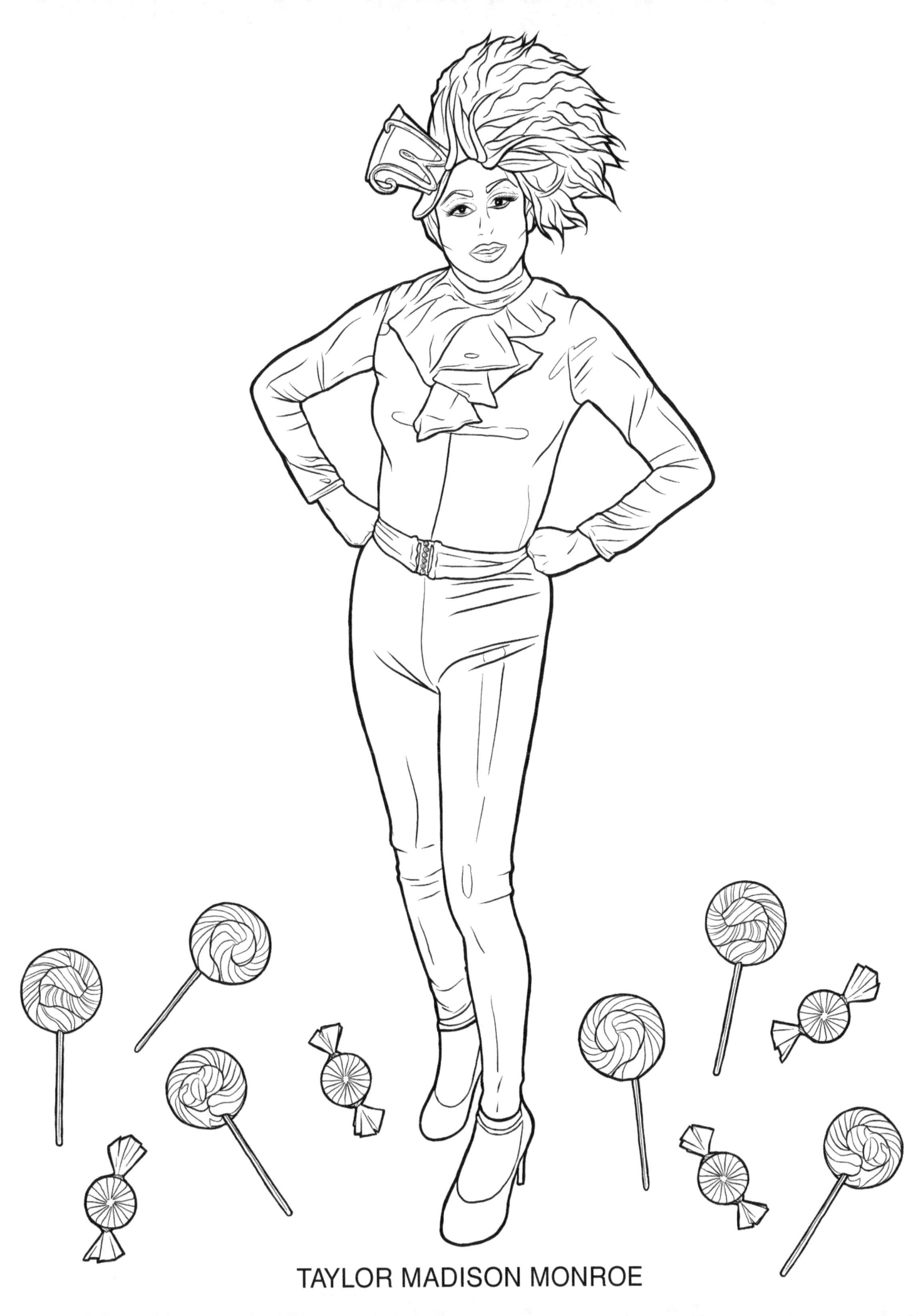

TAYLOR MADISON MONROE

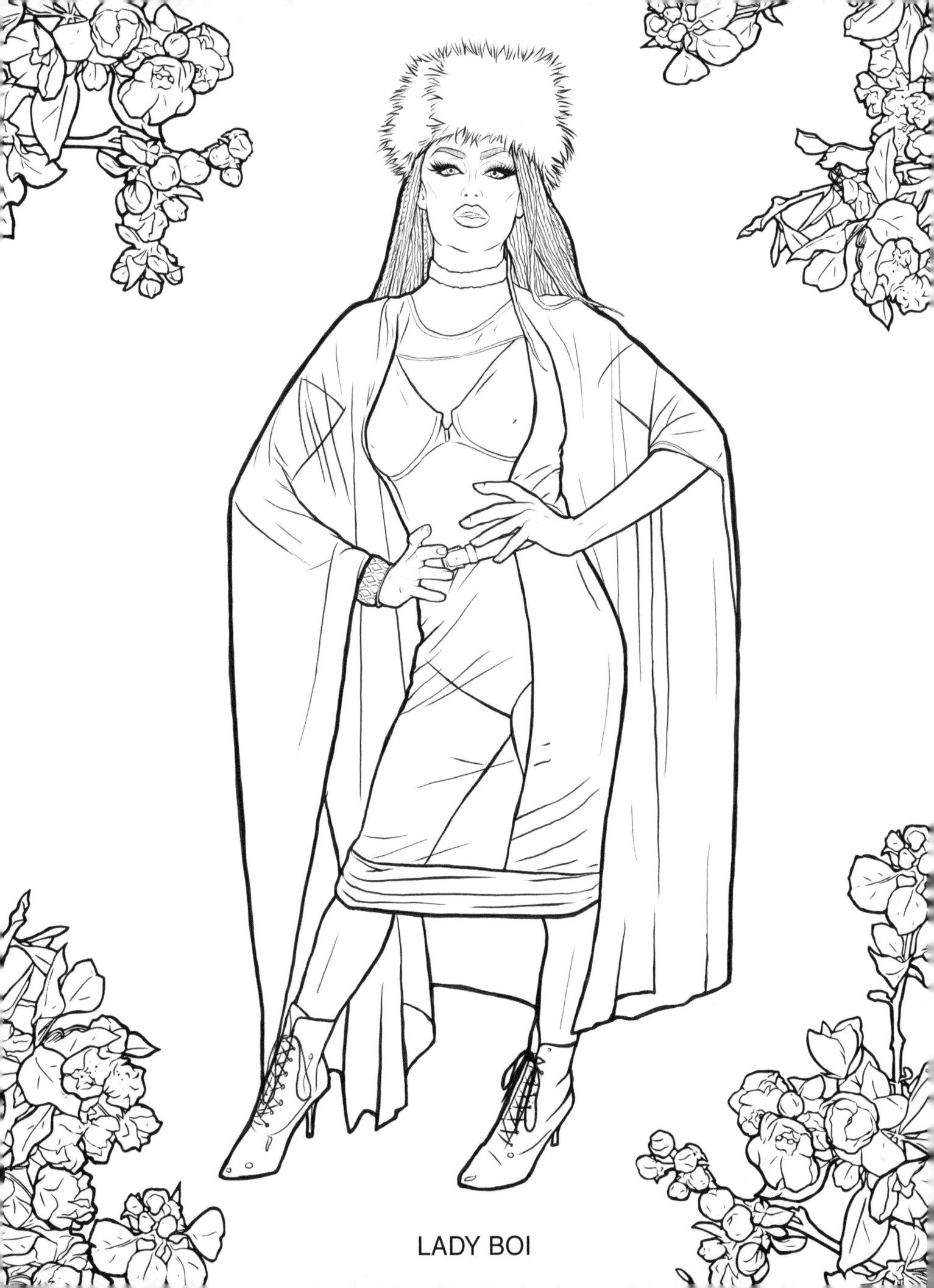

LADY BOI

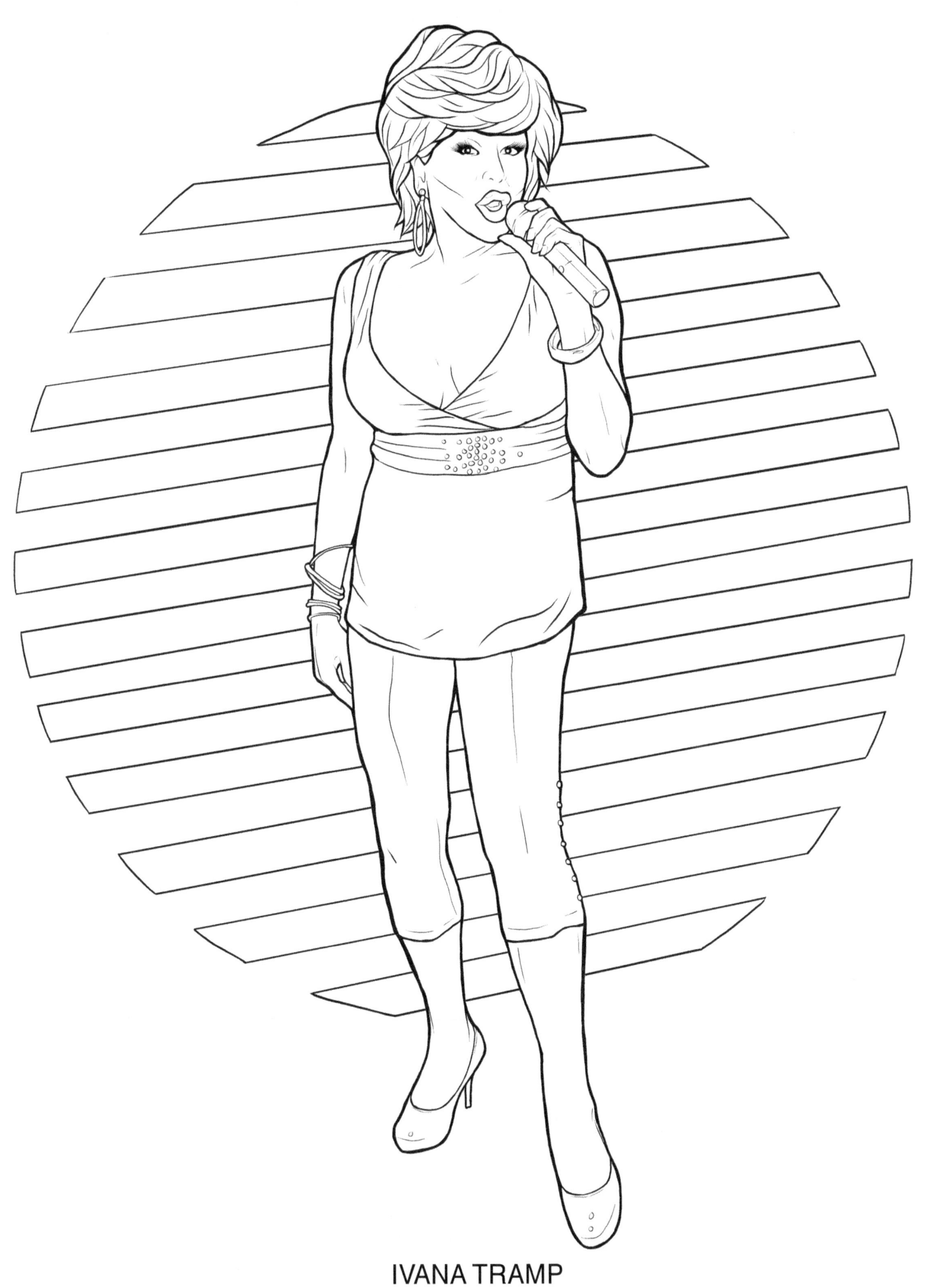

IVANA TRAMP

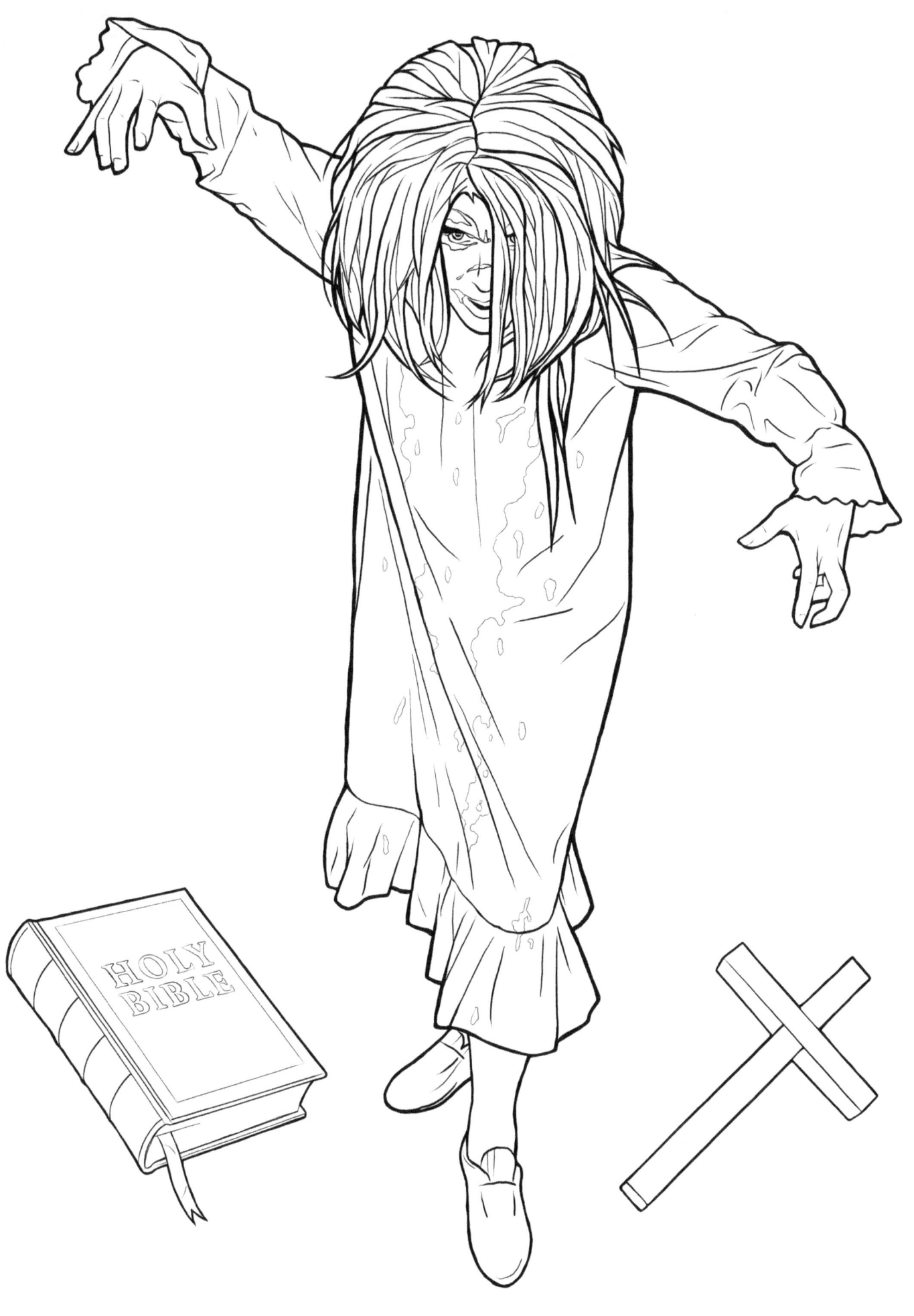

EDEN ALIVE

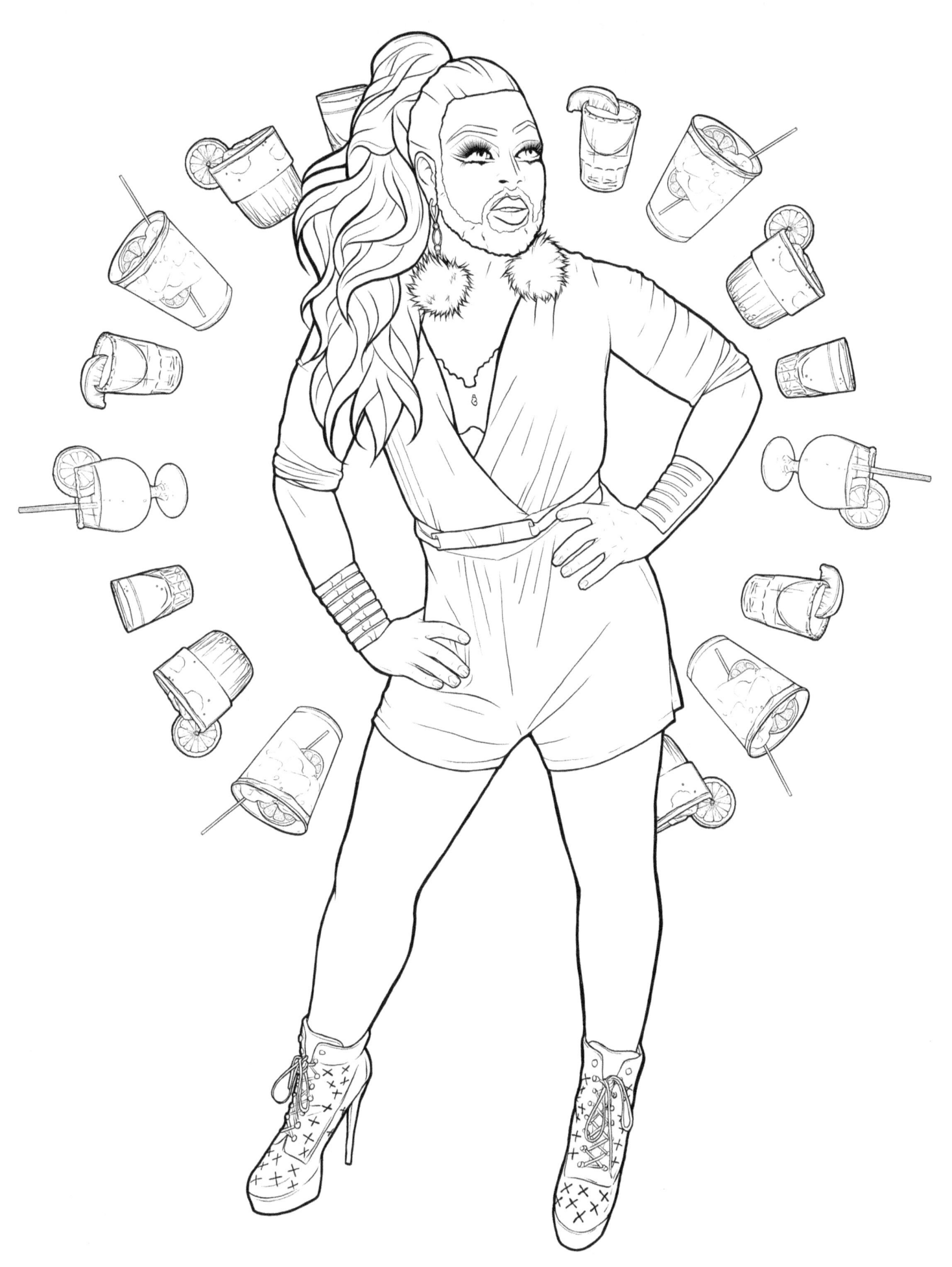

ENVY S HART

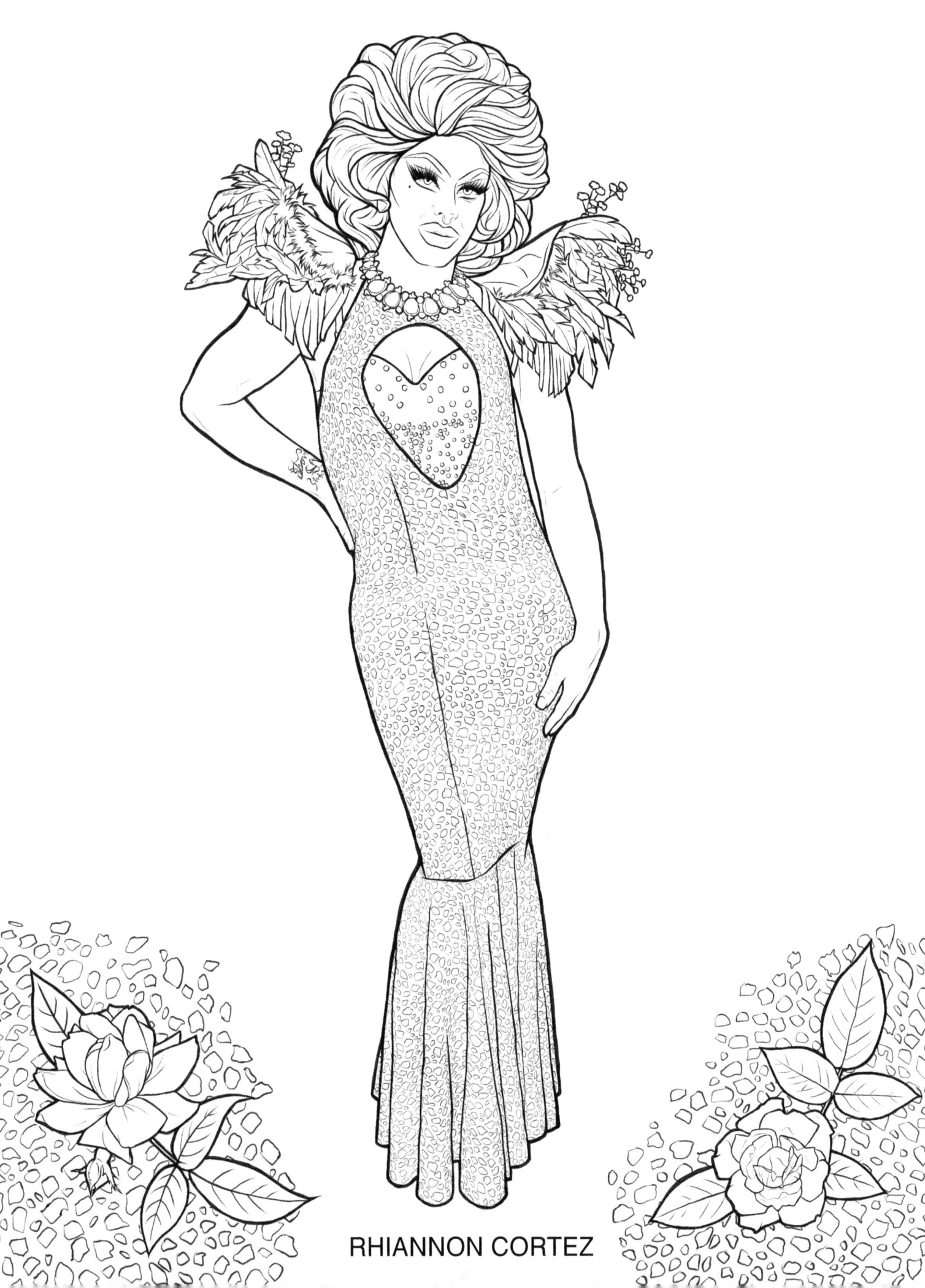

RHIANNON CORTEZ

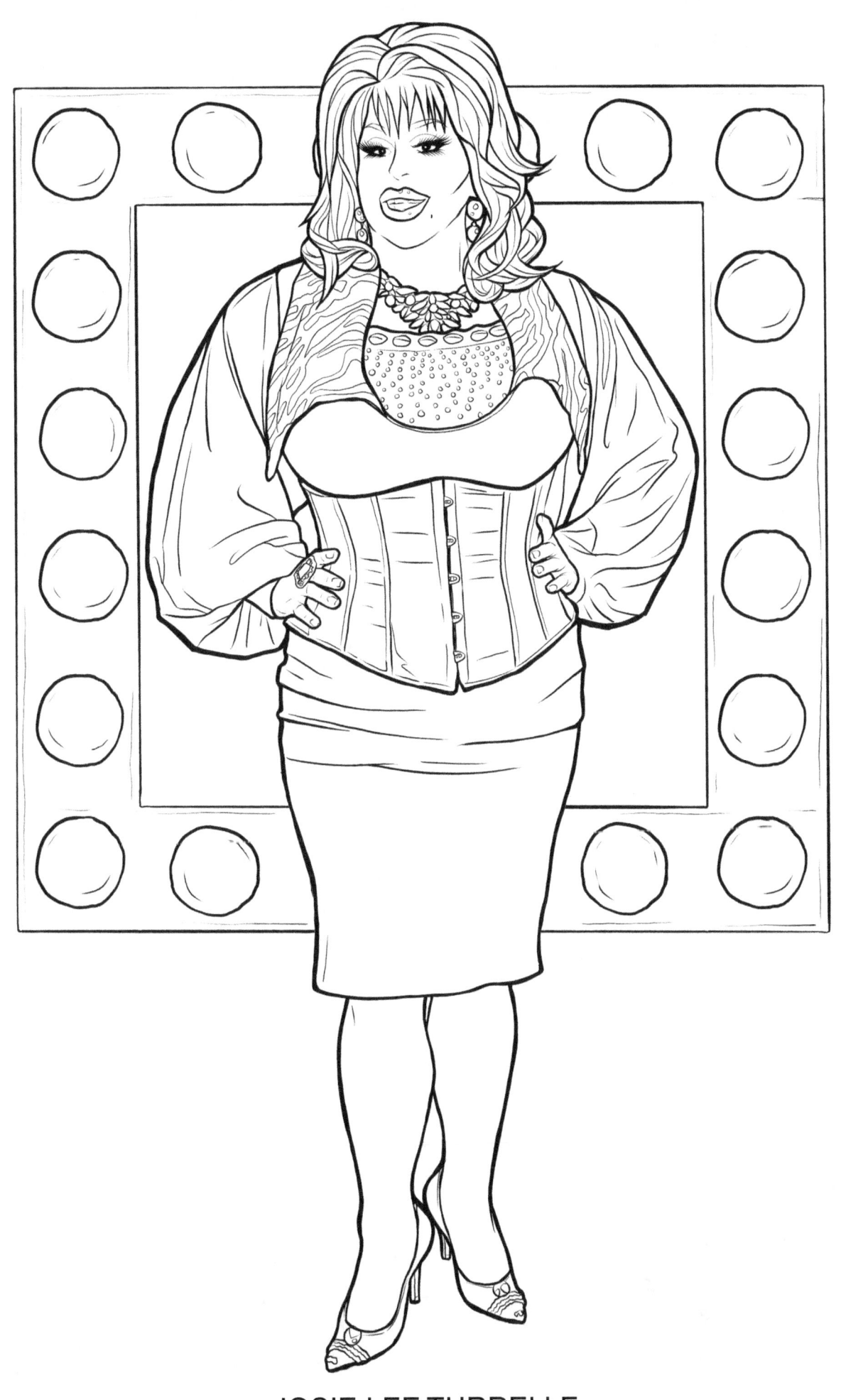

JOSIE LEE TURRELLE

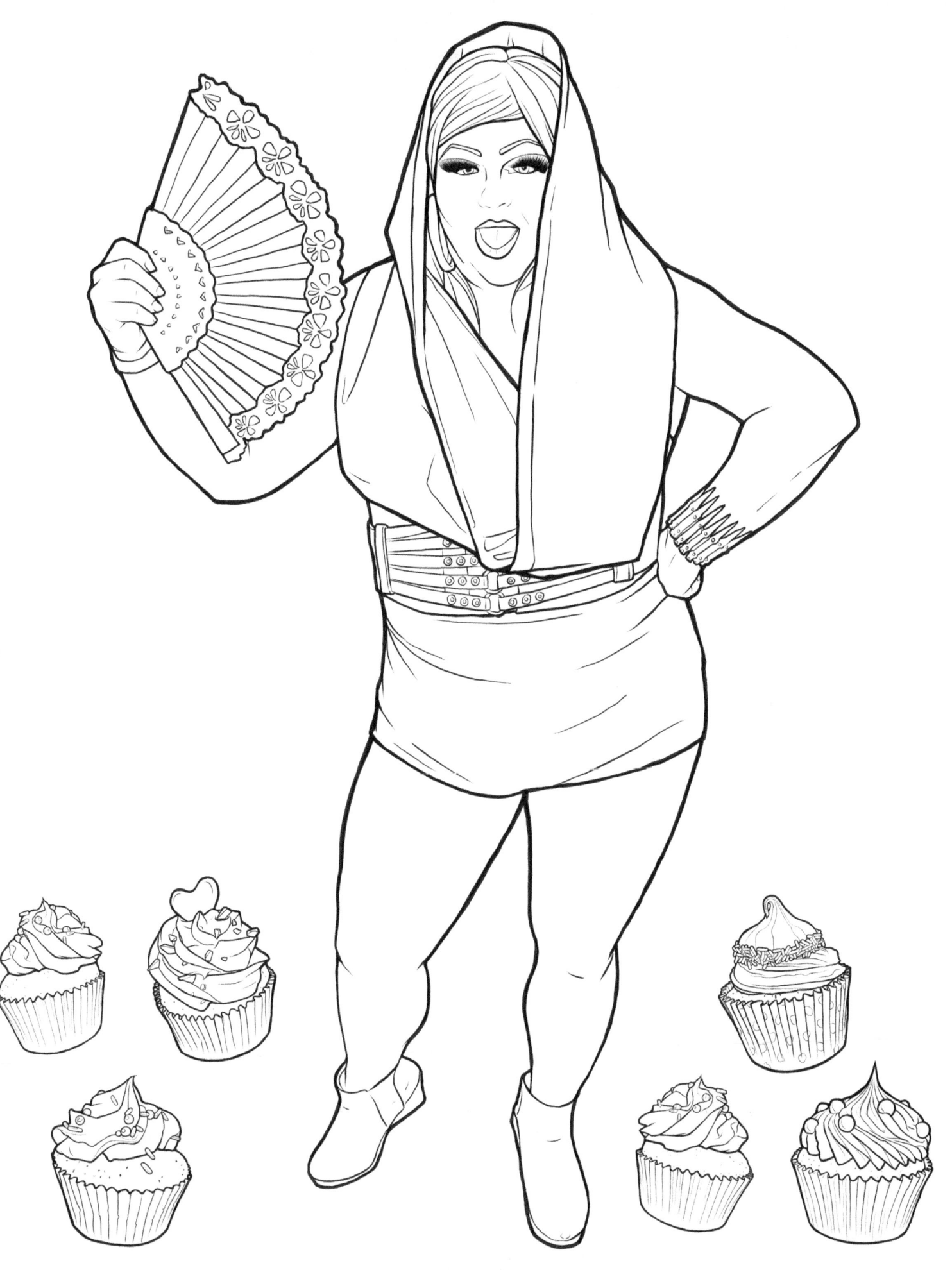

LADY KAKES MONROE

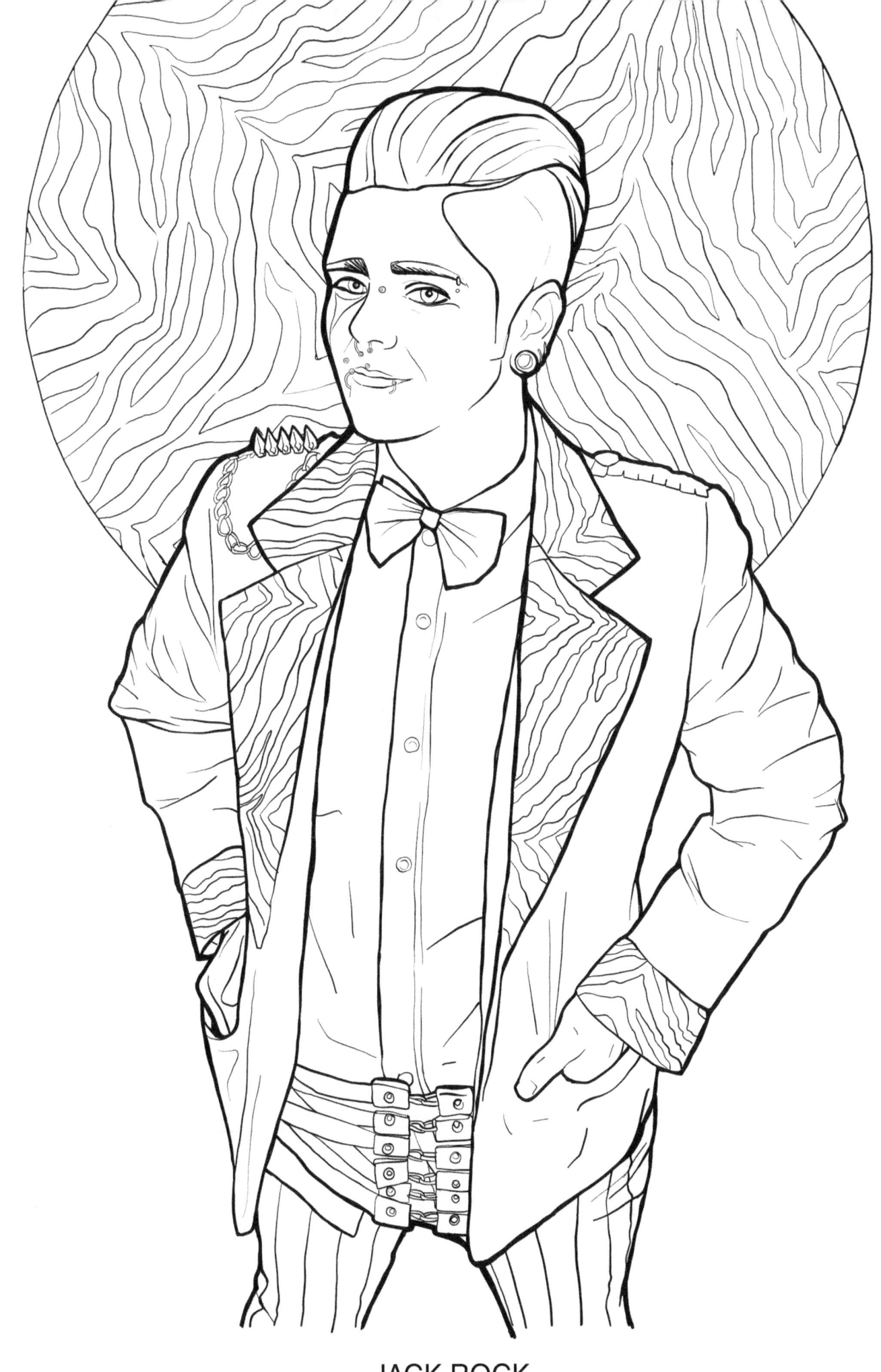

JACK ROCK

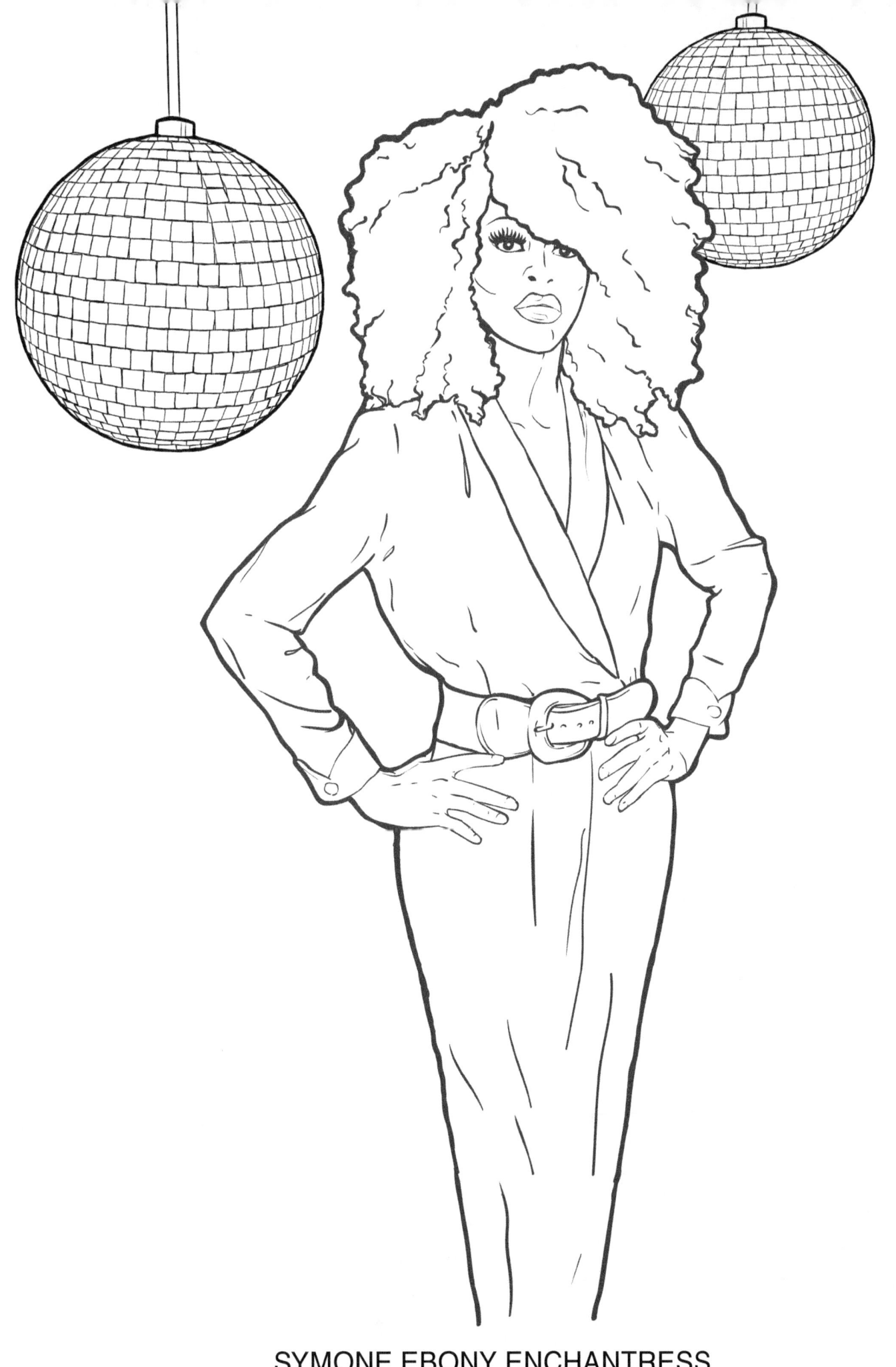

SYMONE EBONY ENCHANTRESS

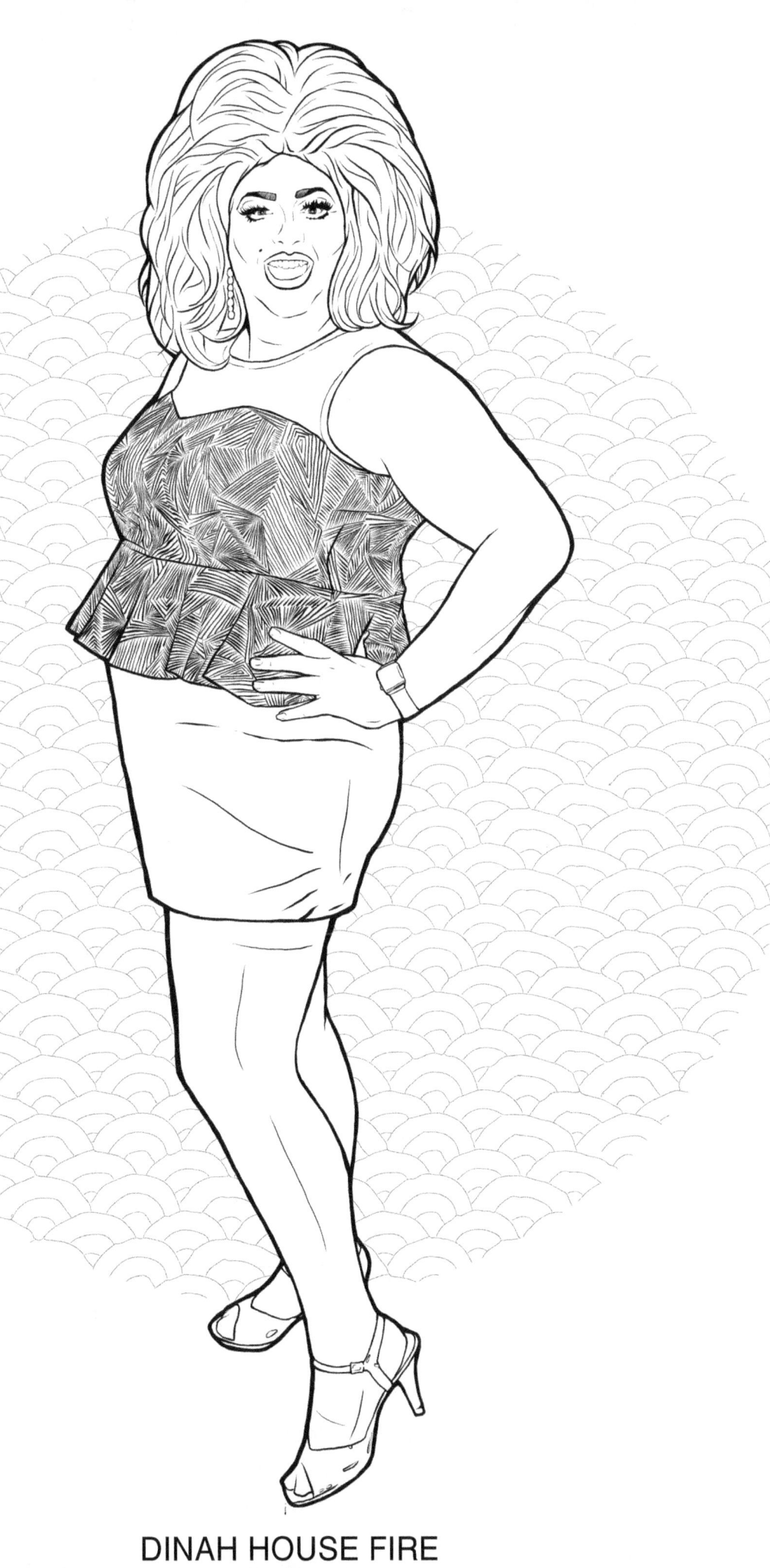

DINAH HOUSE FIRE

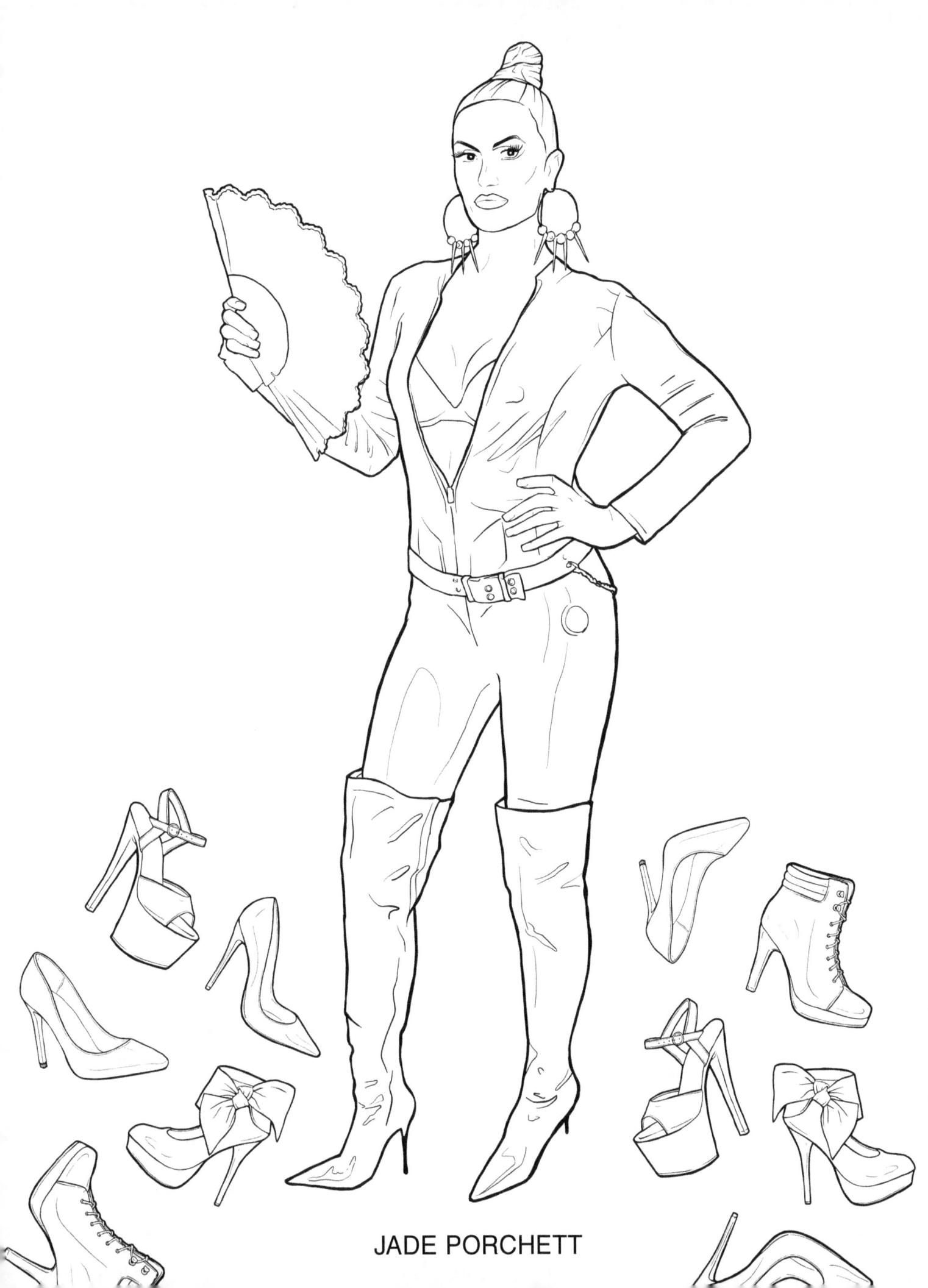

JADE PORCHETT

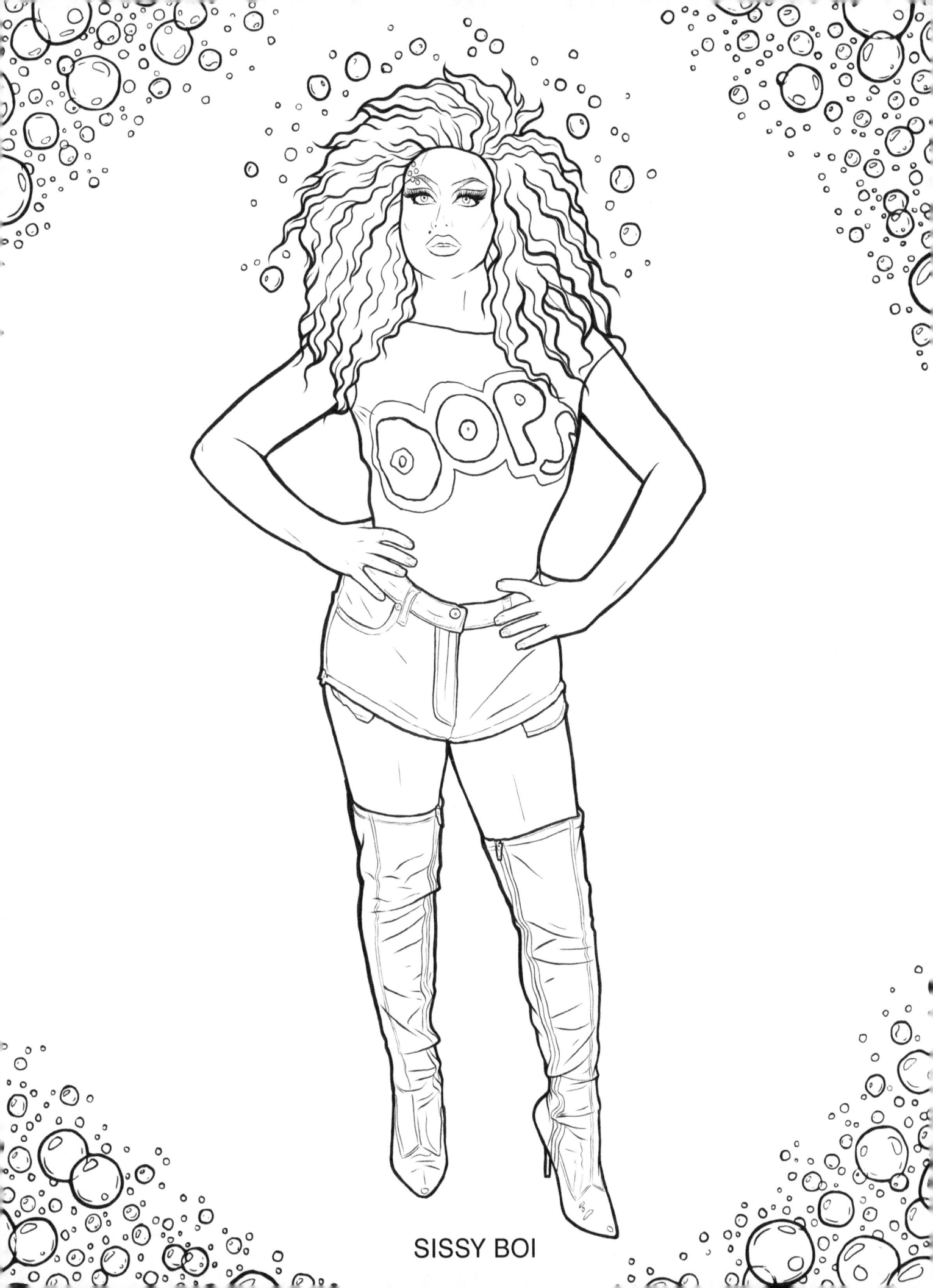

SISSY BOI

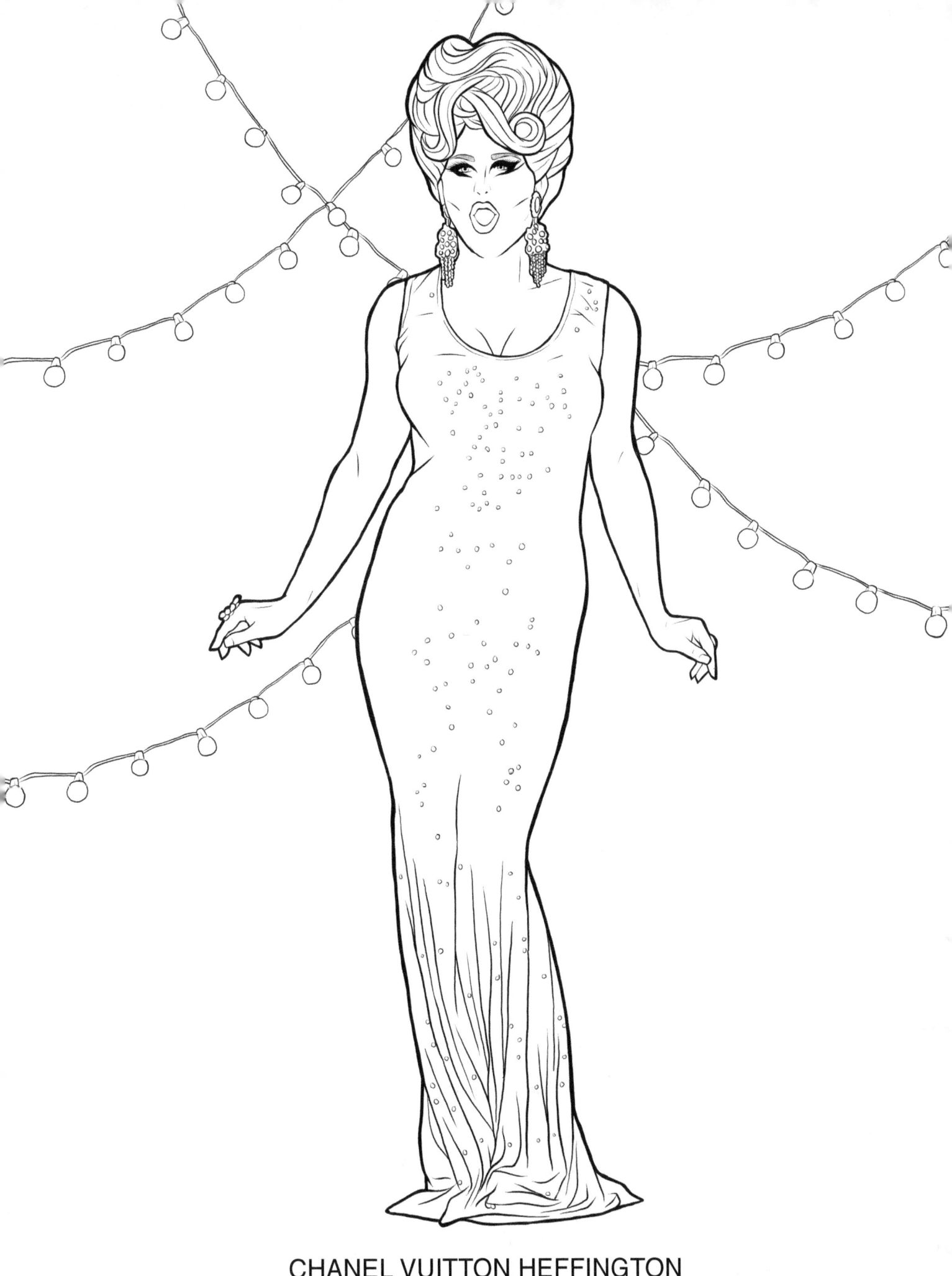

CHANEL VUITTON HEFFINGTON

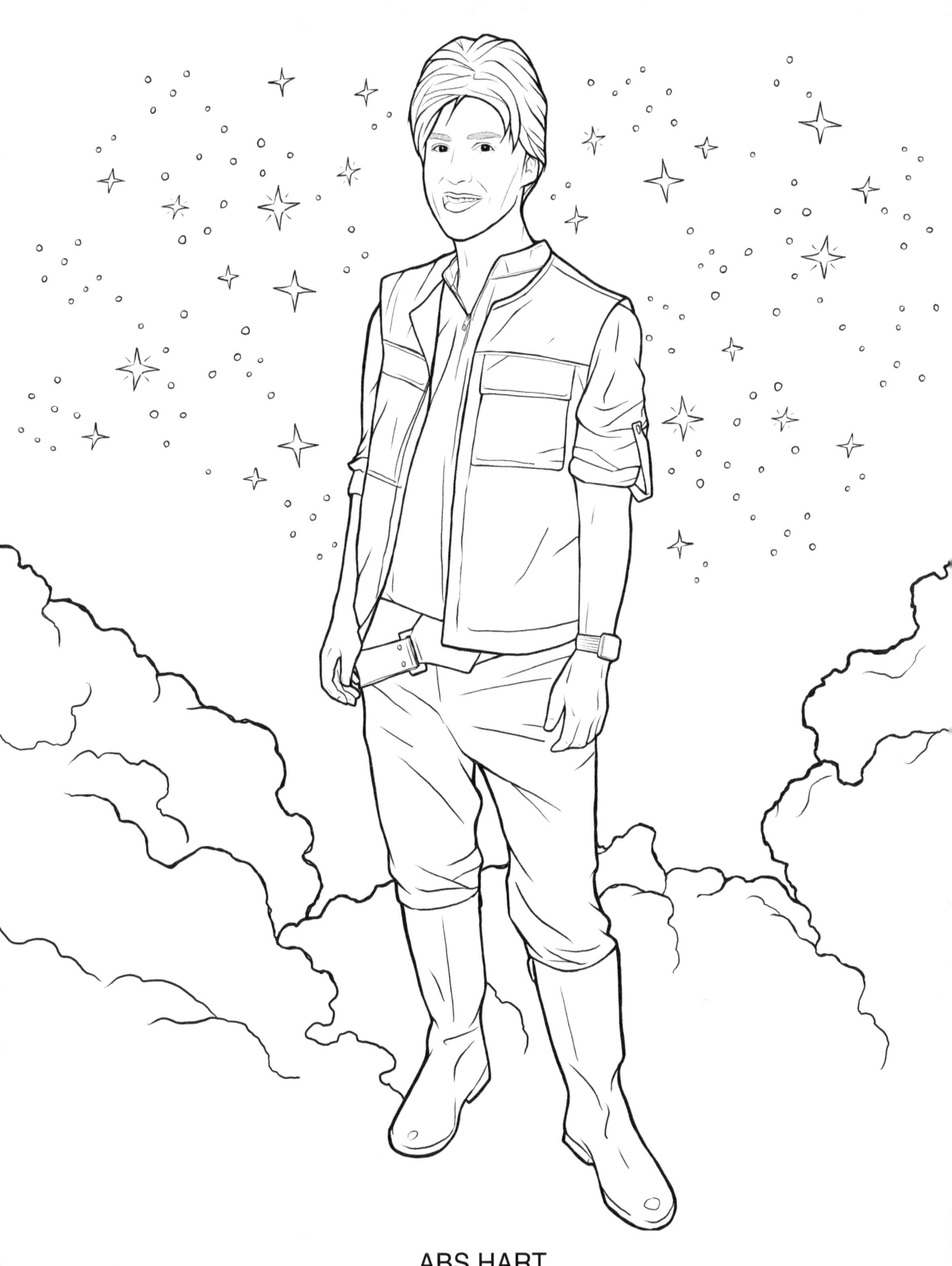

ABS HART

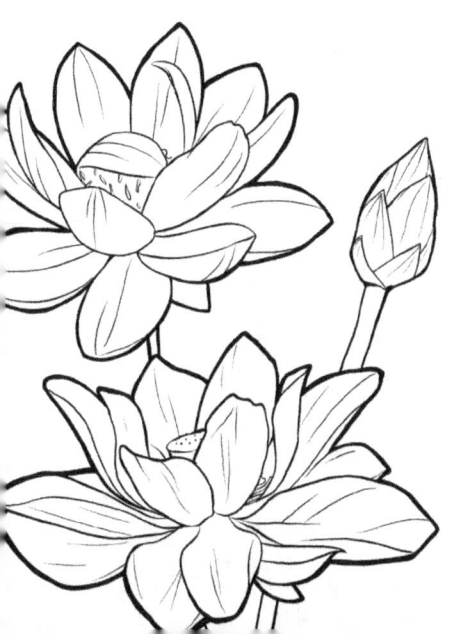

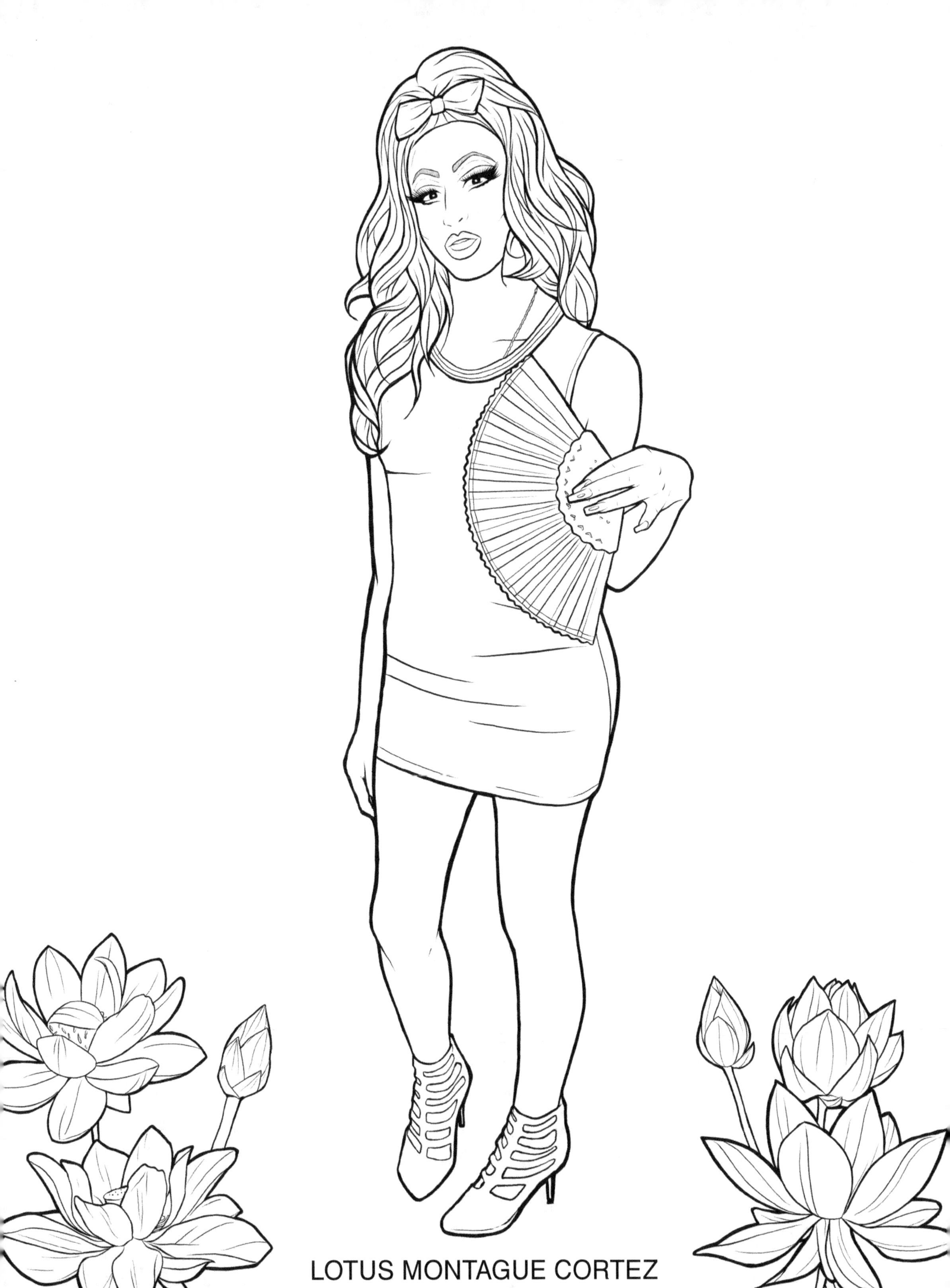

LOTUS MONTAGUE CORTEZ

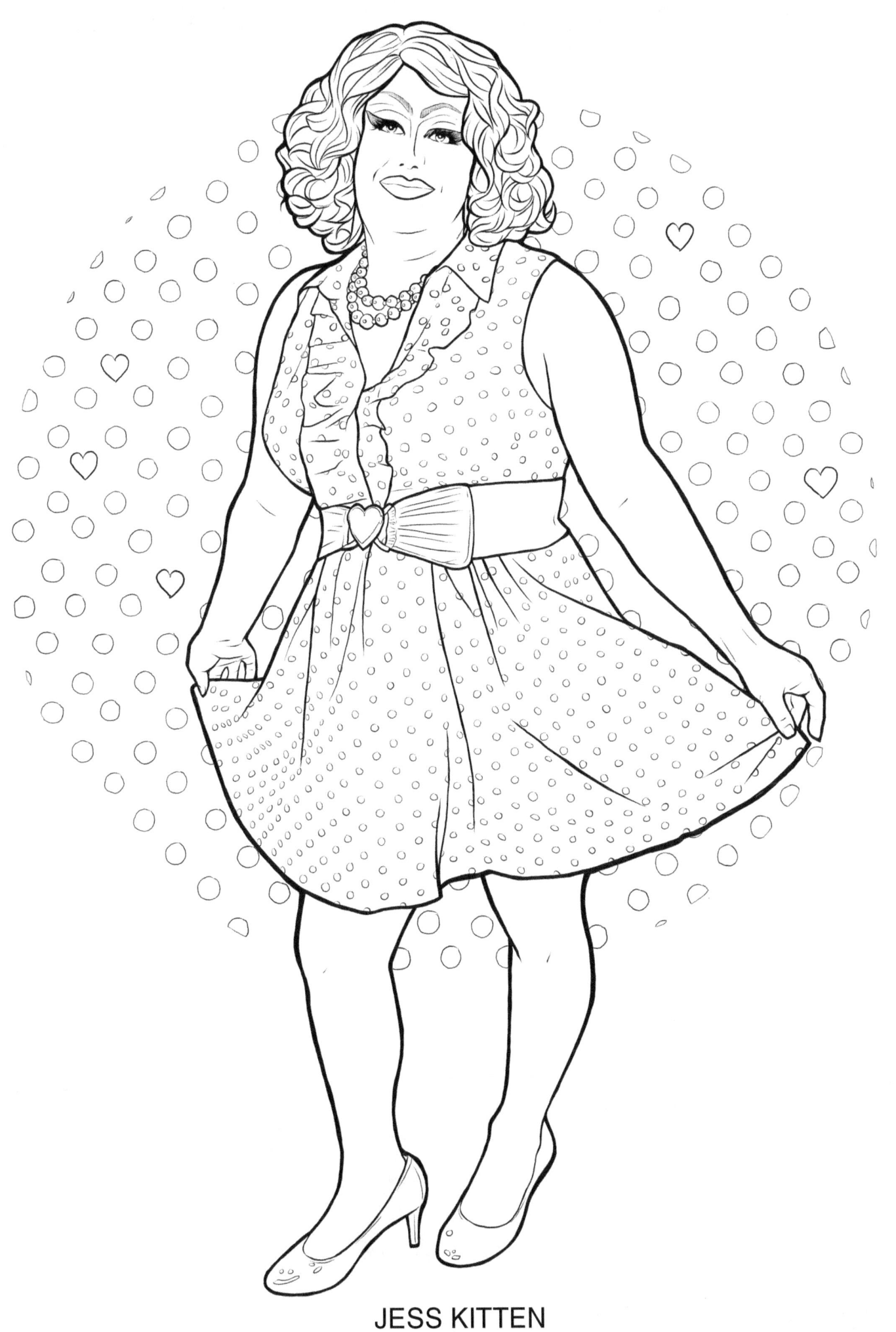

JESS KITTEN

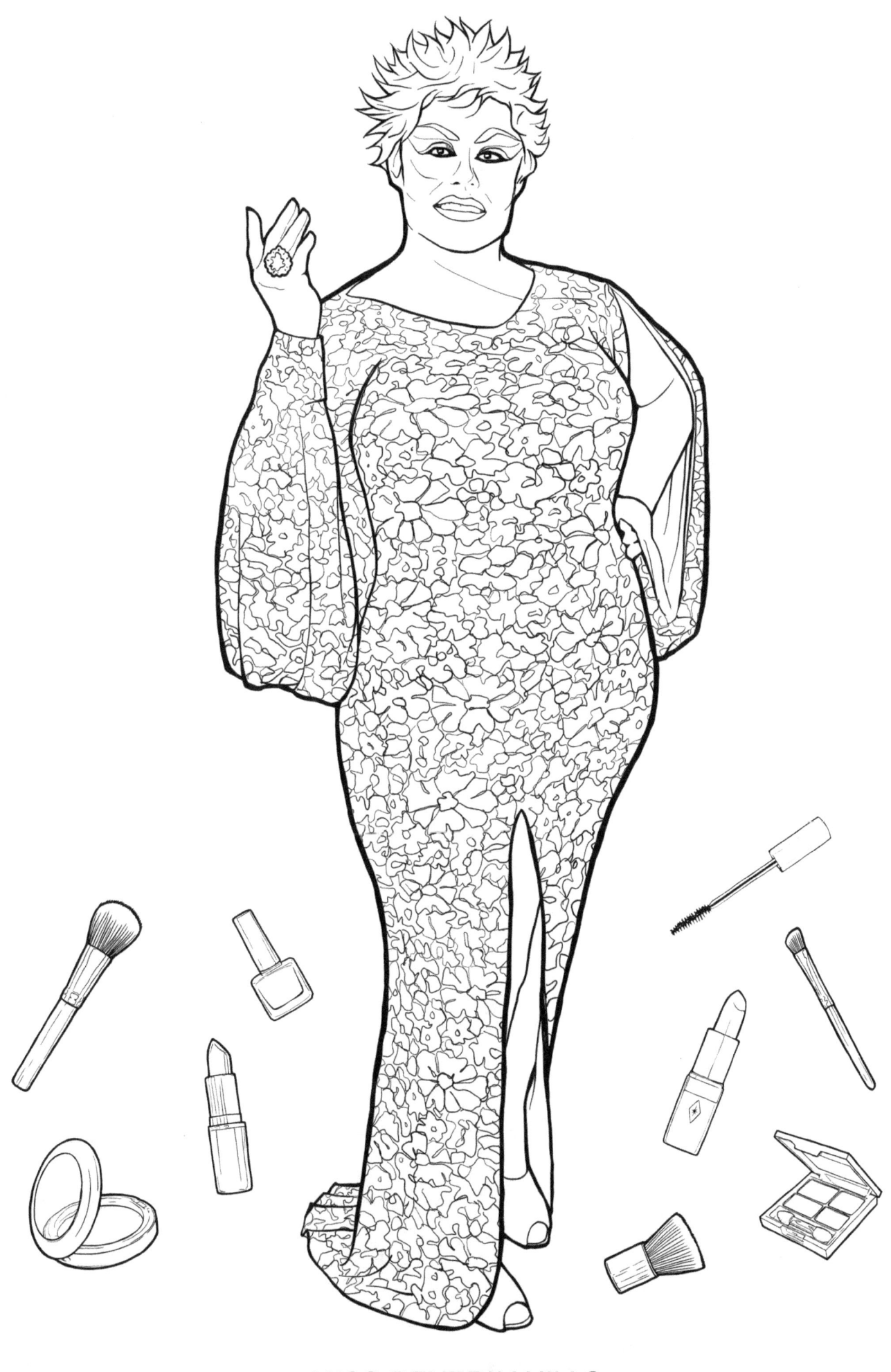

MISS BEVERLY HILLS

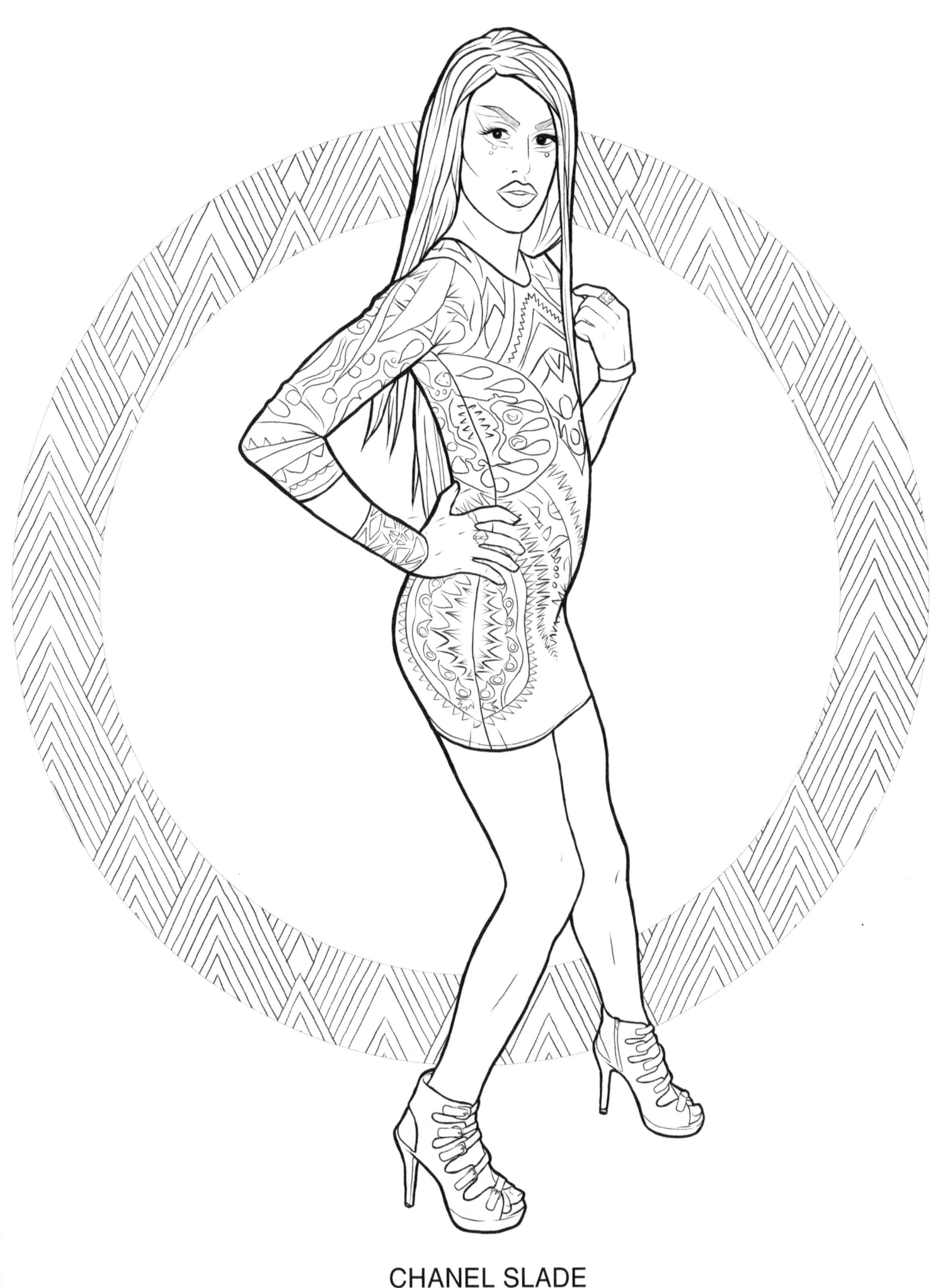

CHANEL SLADE

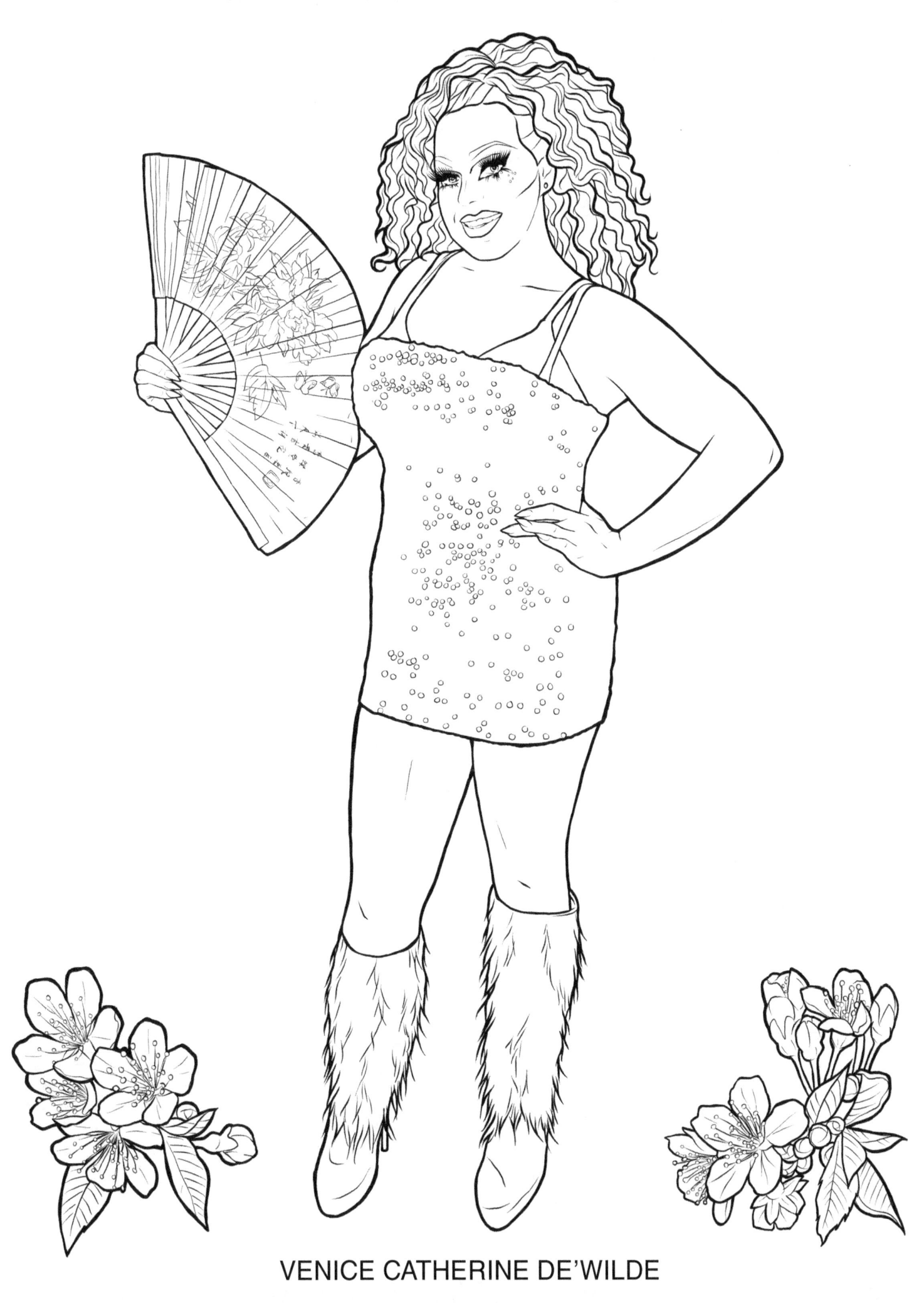

VENICE CATHERINE DE'WILDE

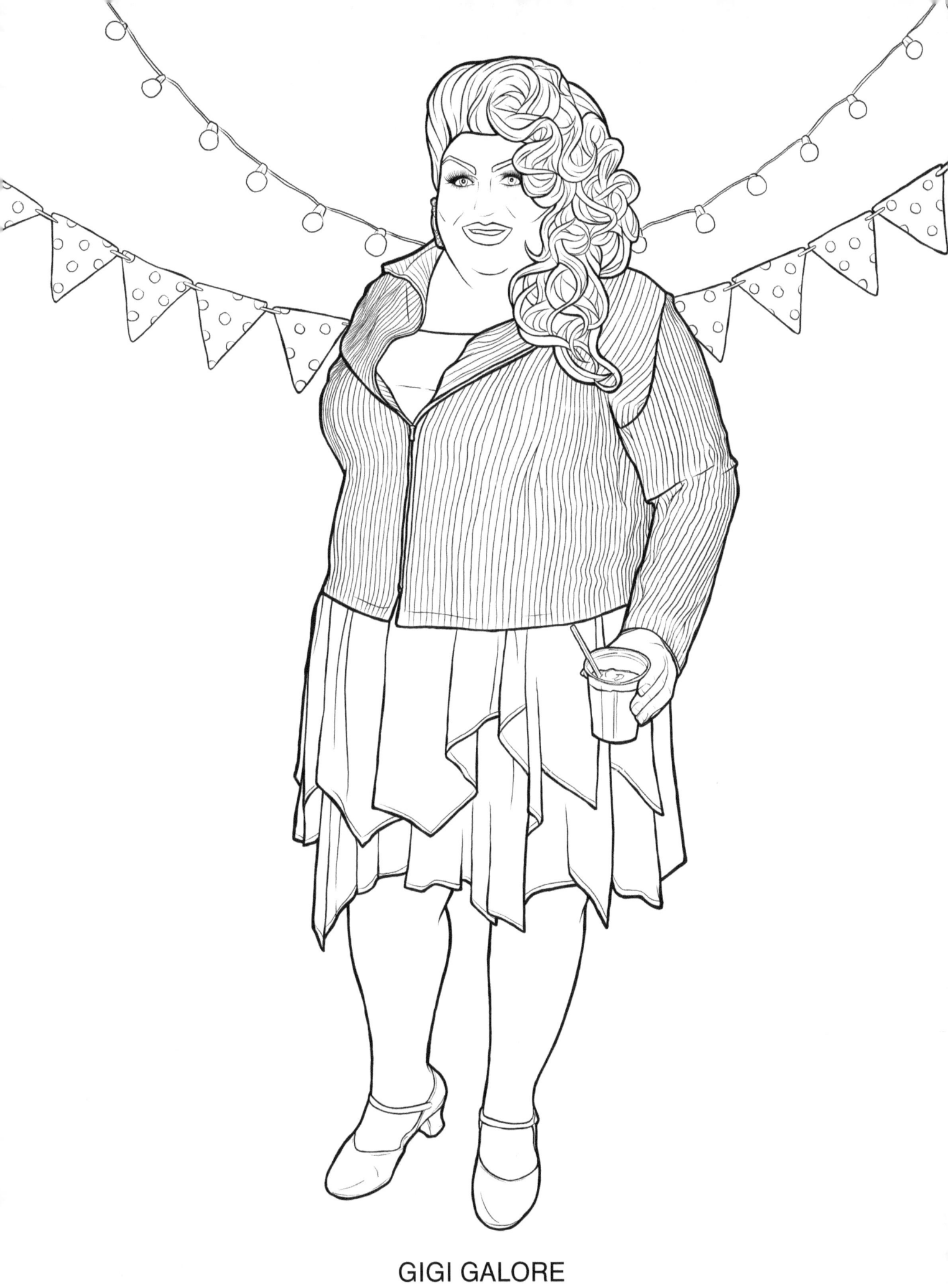

GIGI GALORE

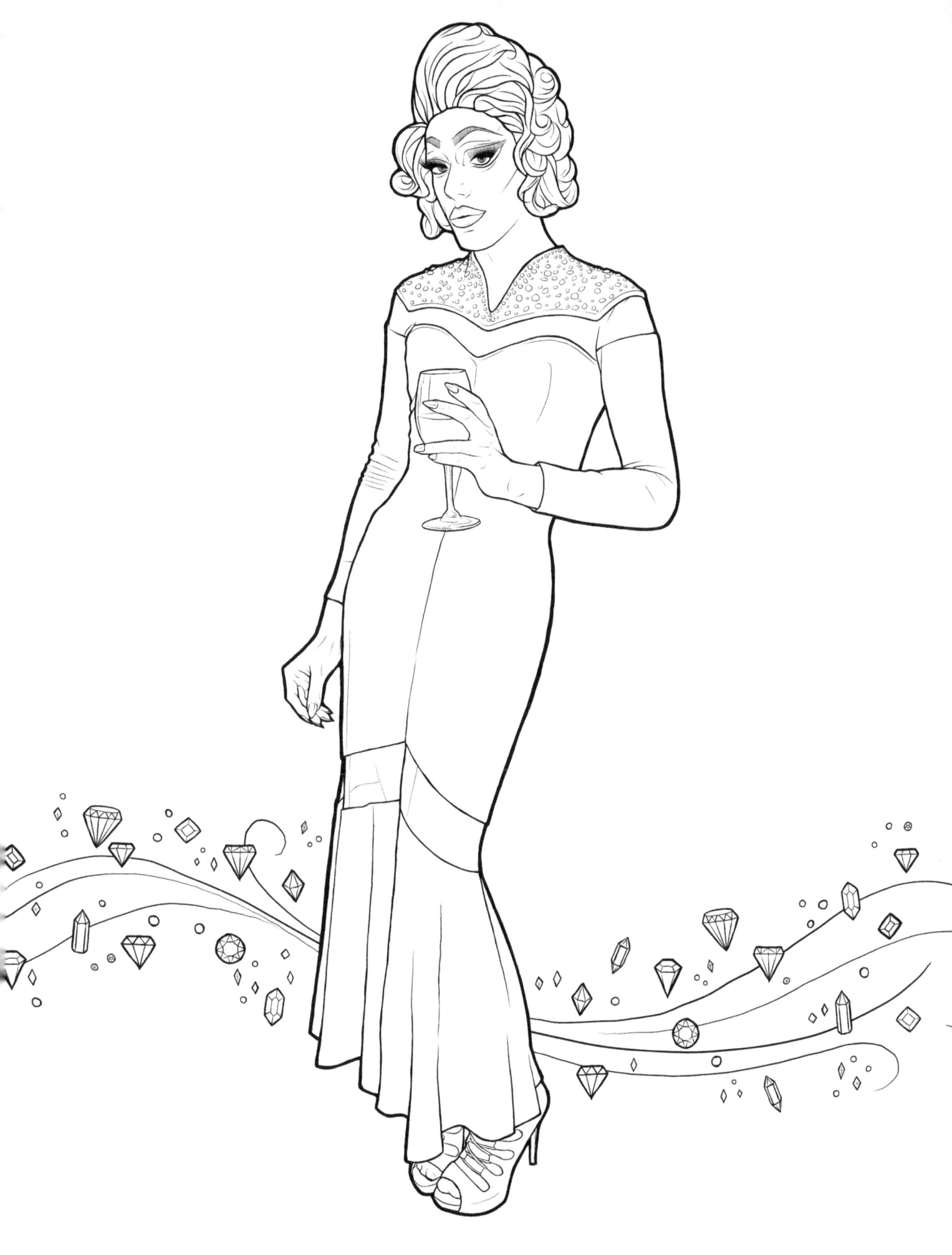

AUDREY CORTEZ

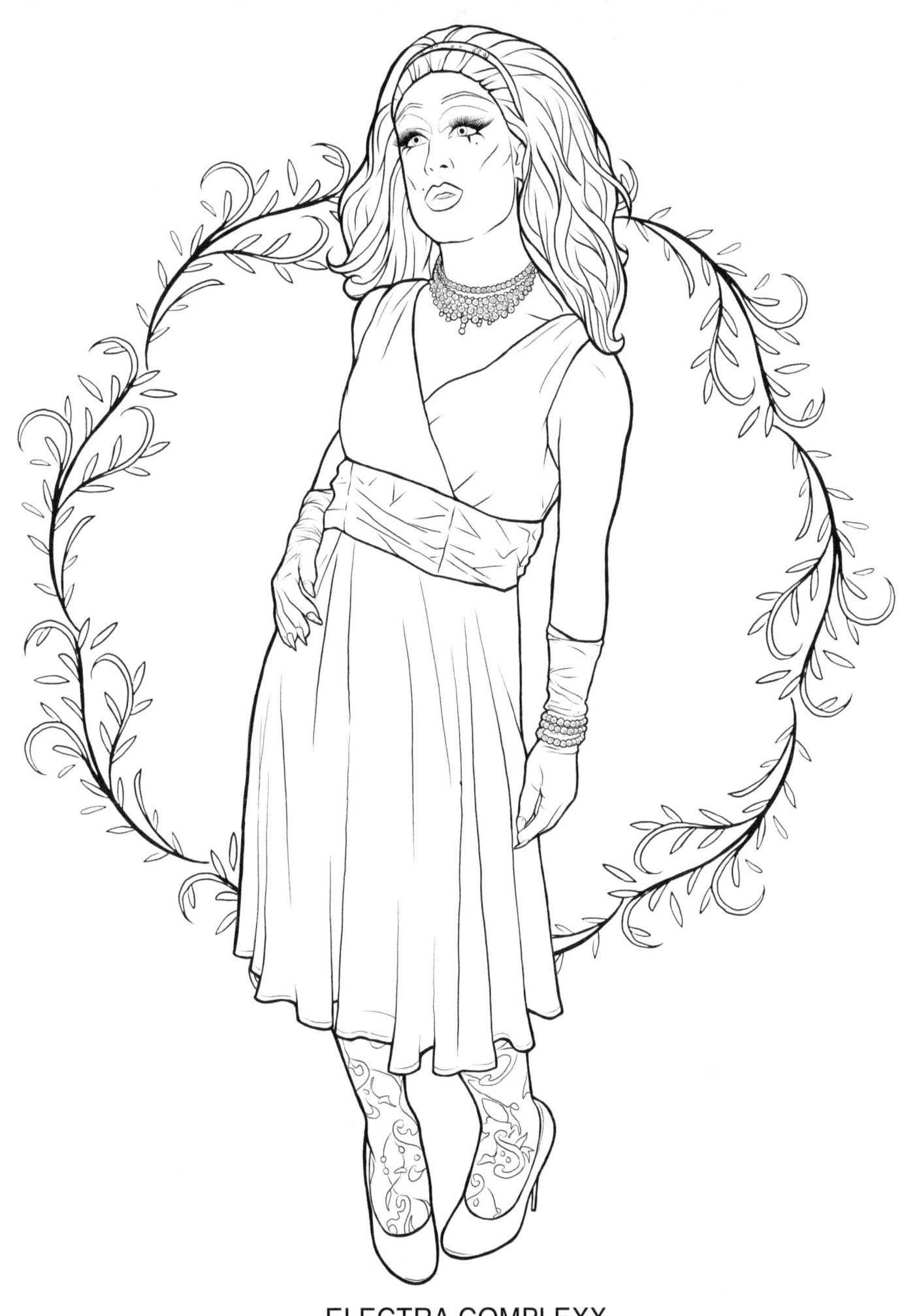

ELECTRA COMPLEXX

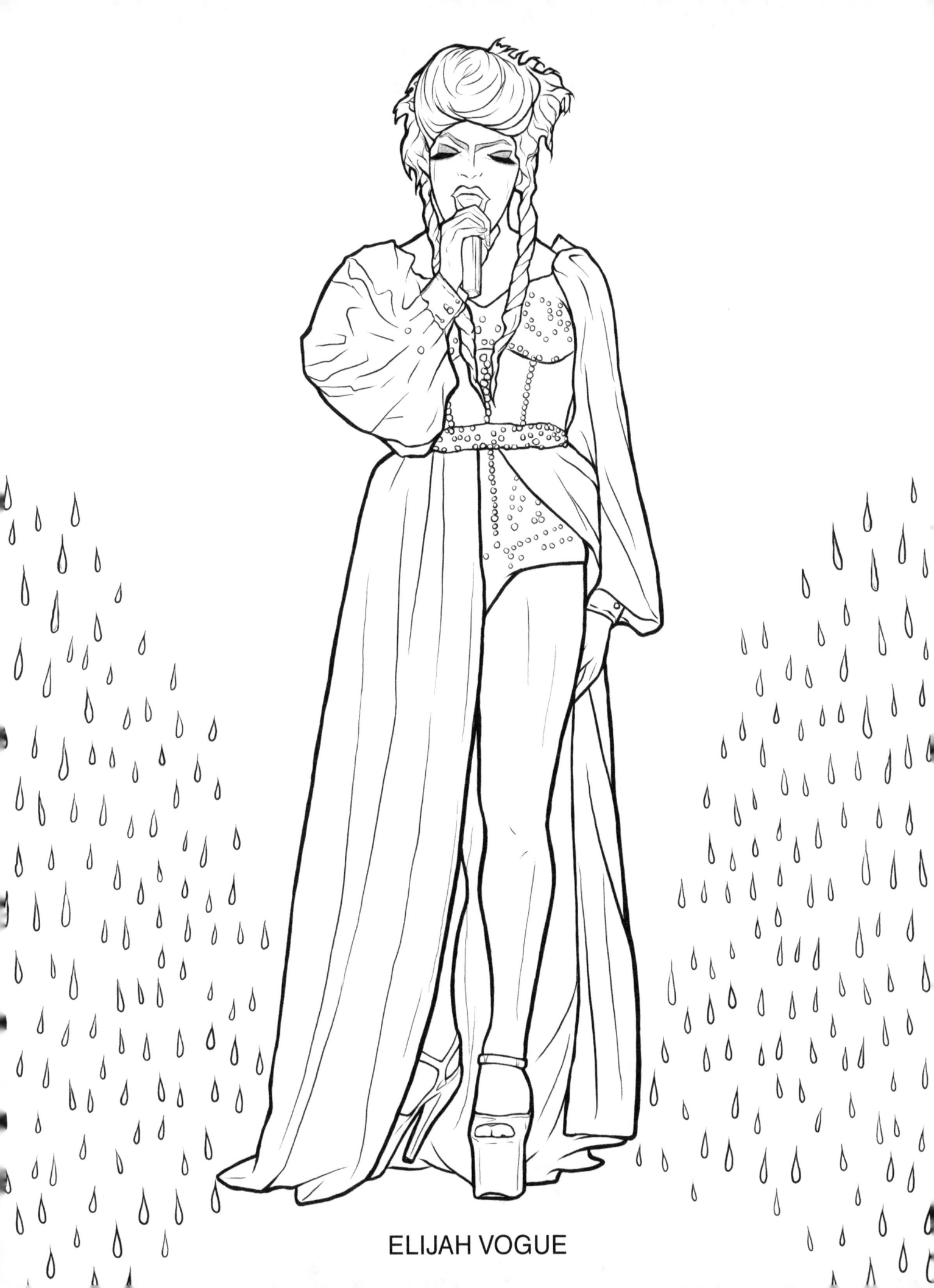

ELIJAH VOGUE

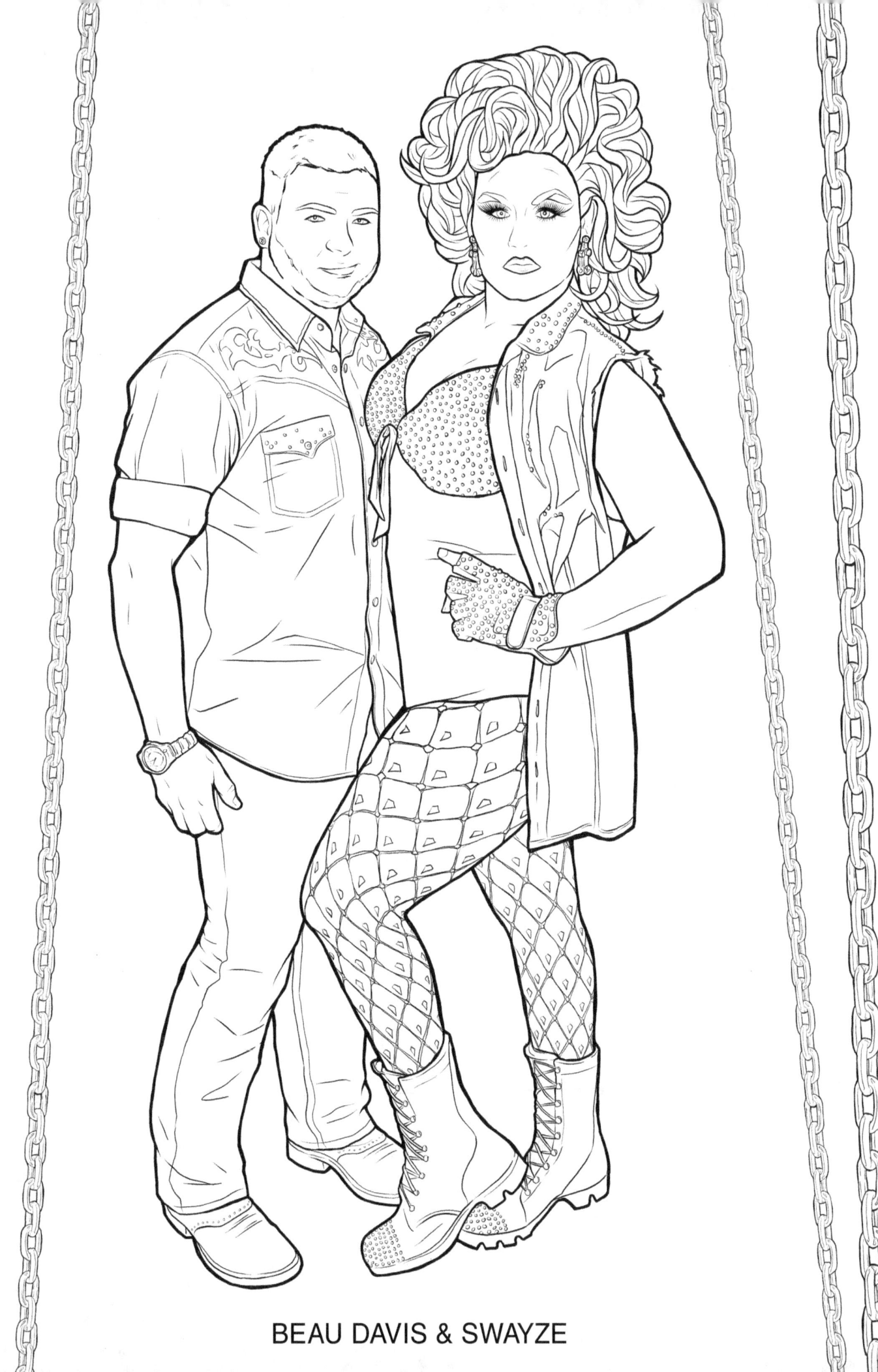

BEAU DAVIS & SWAYZE

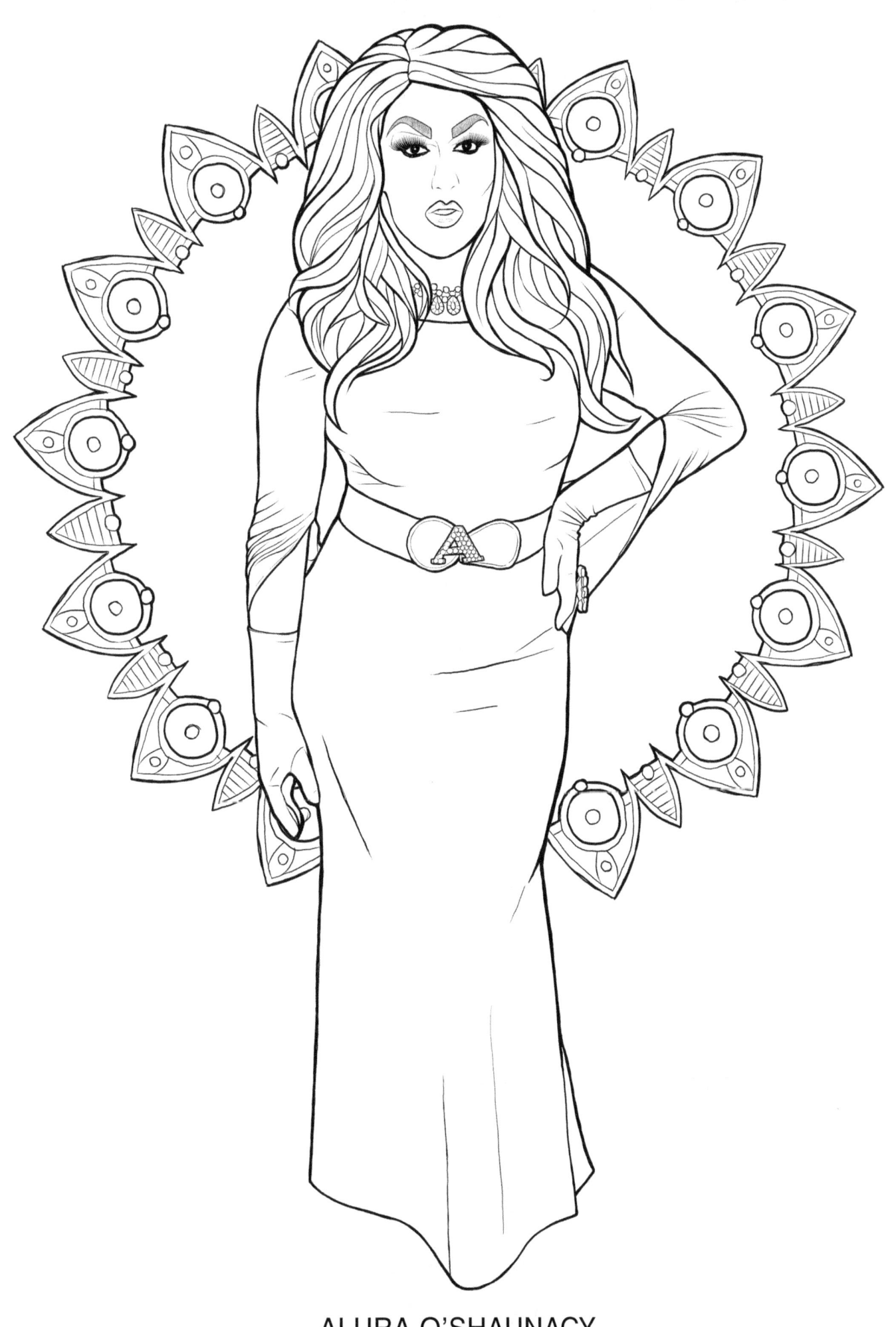

ALURA O'SHAUNACY

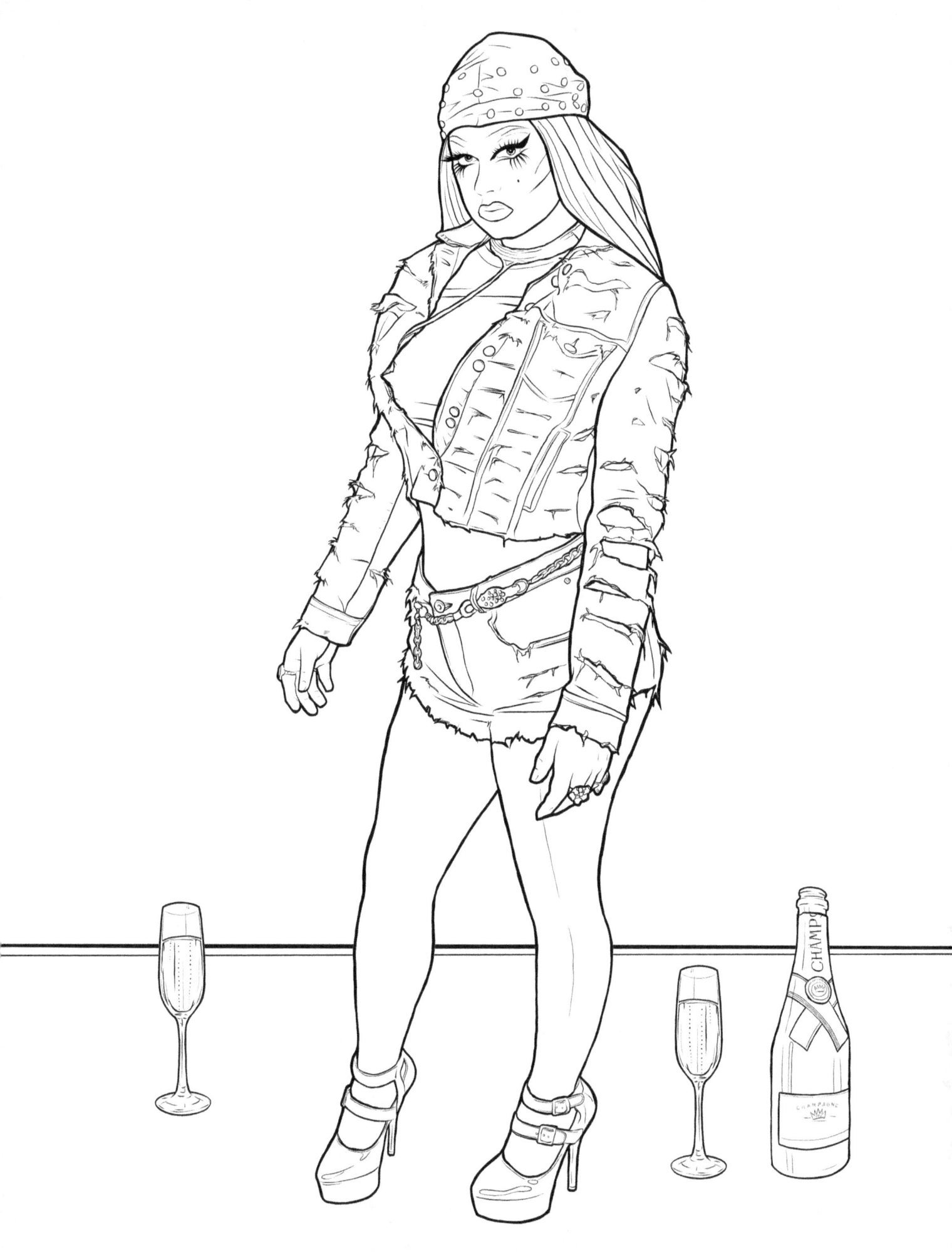

VEGA ST. JAMES

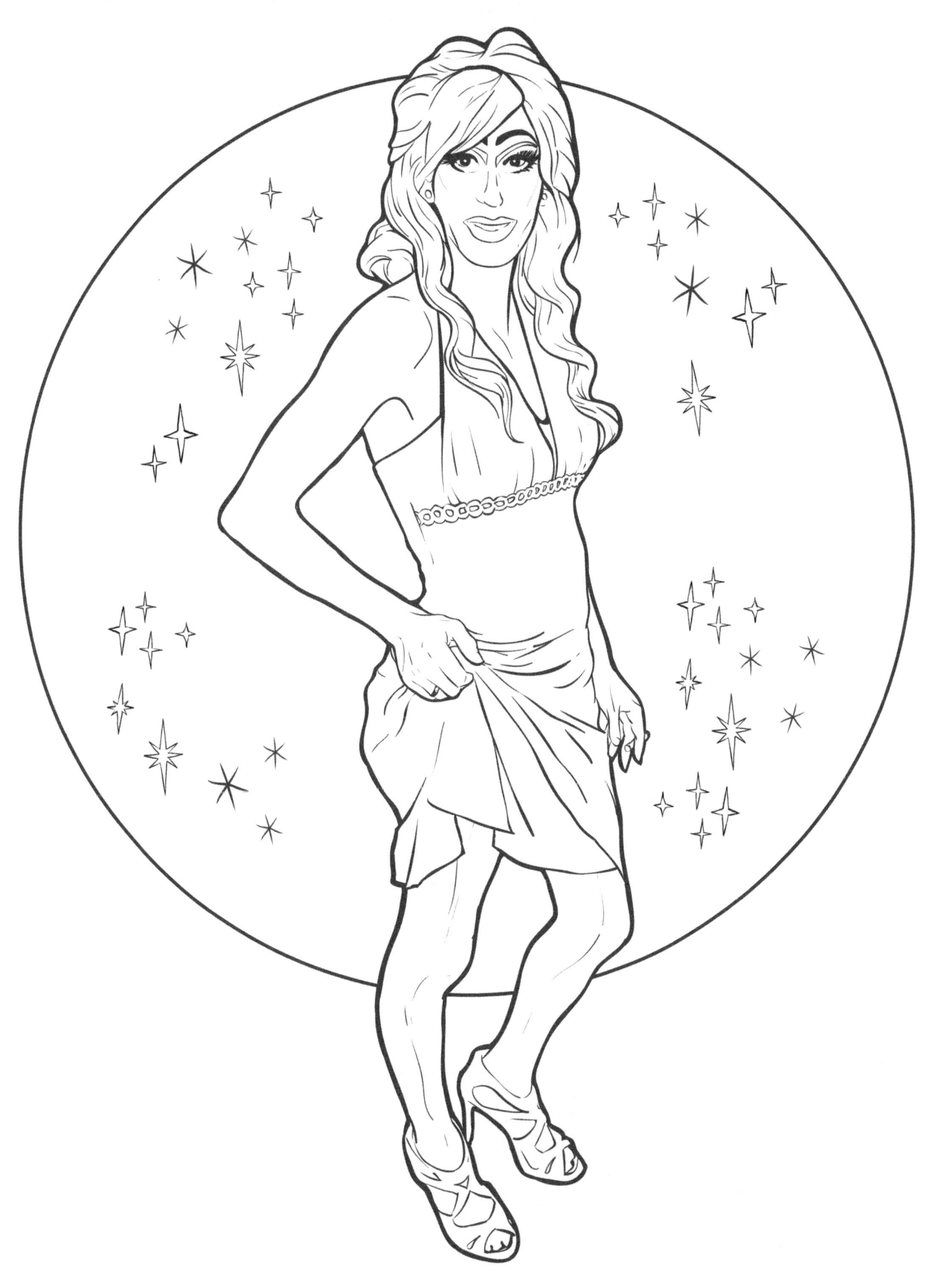

LIL BIT UH HUNNY

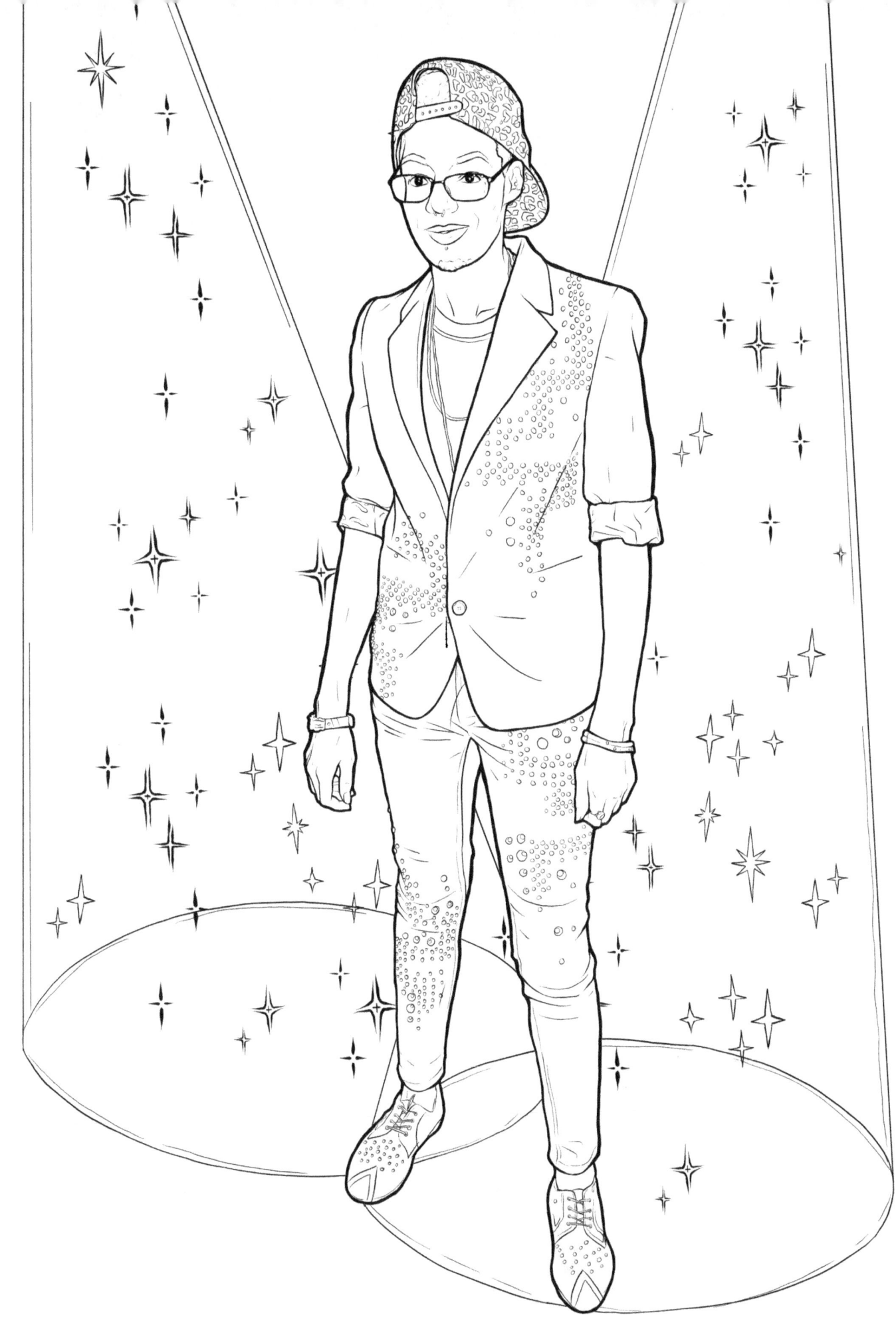

D'ANGELO

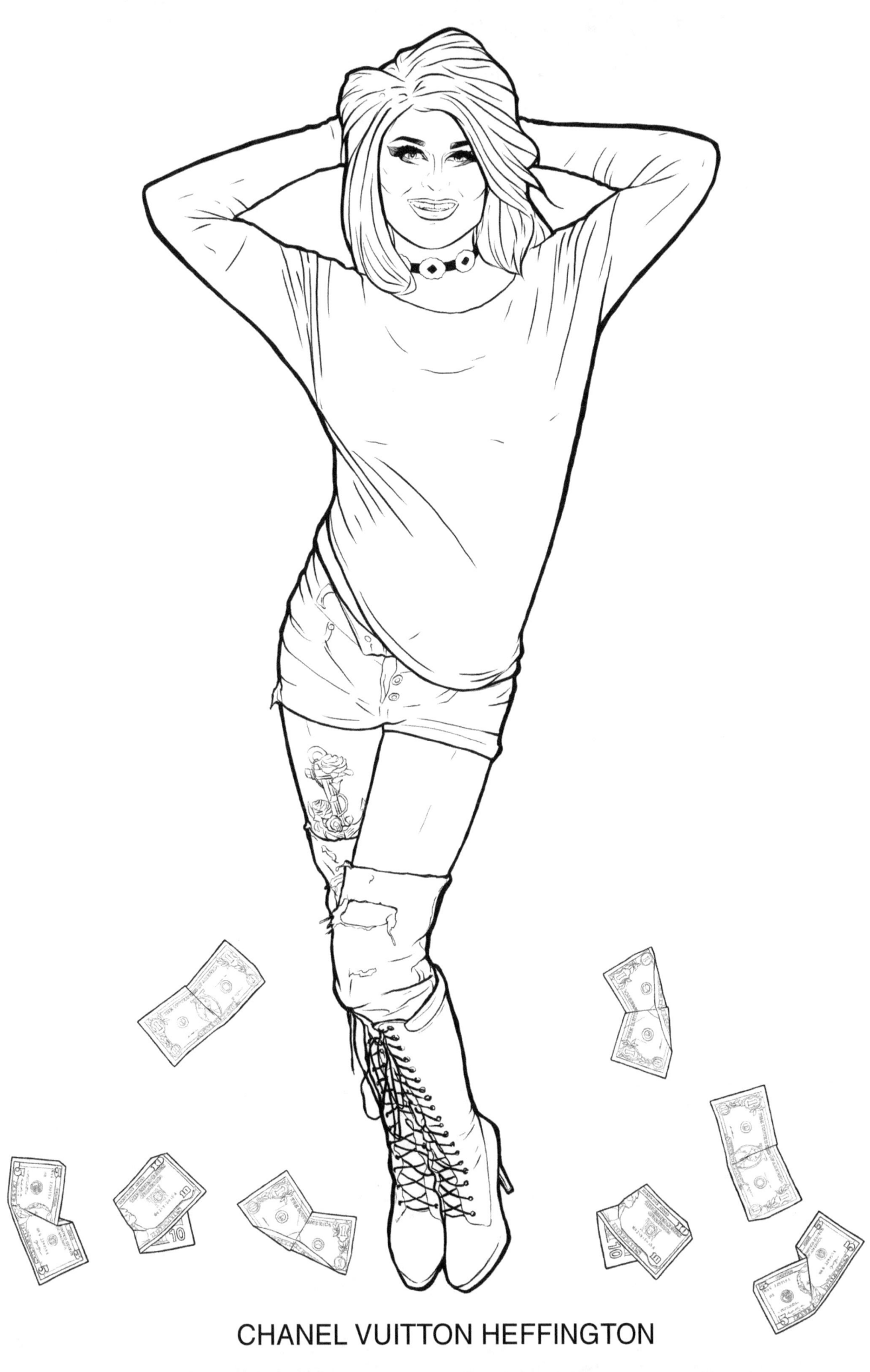

CHANEL VUITTON HEFFINGTON

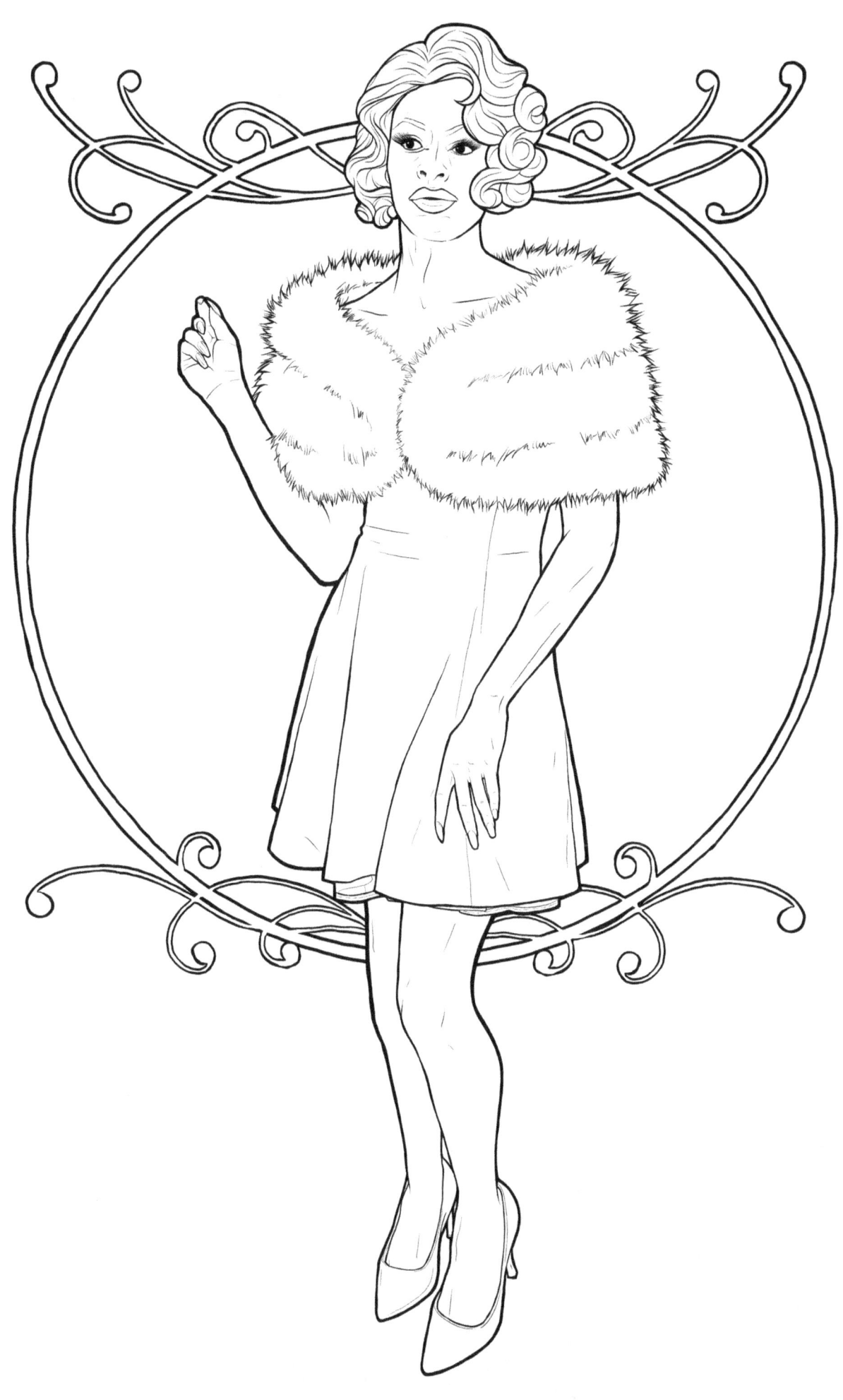

SYMONE EBONY ENCHANTRESS

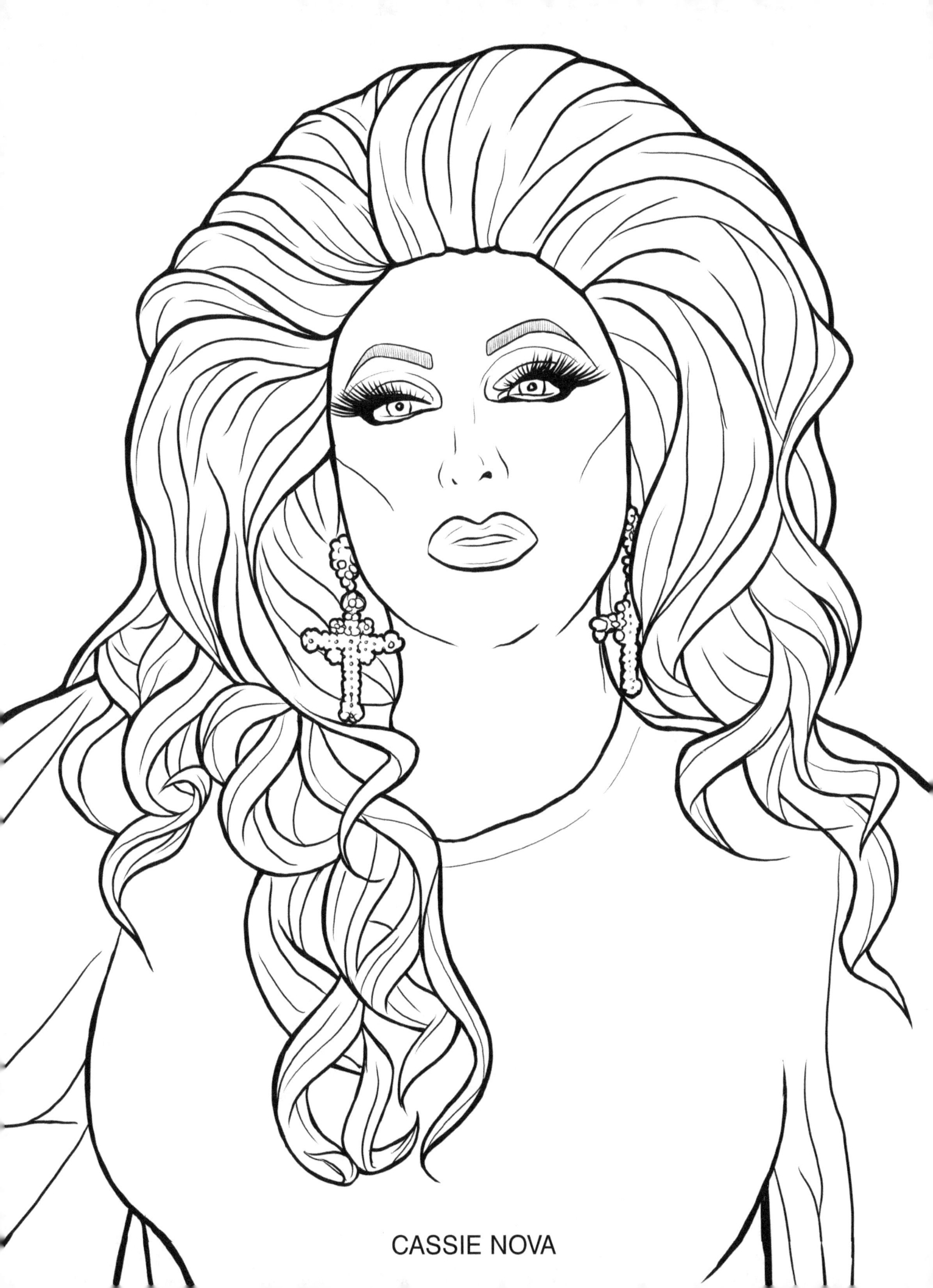

CASSIE NOVA

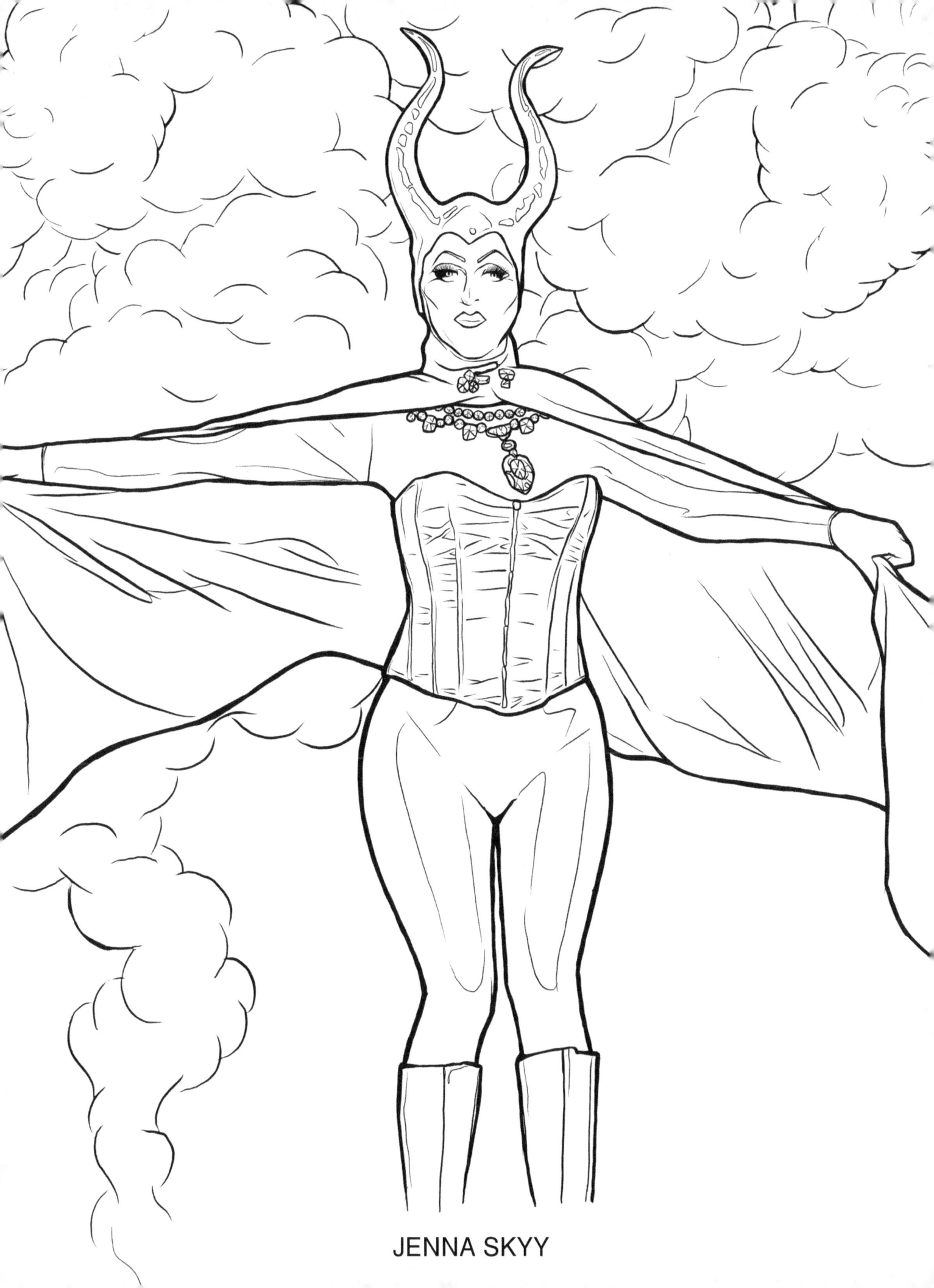

JENNA SKYY

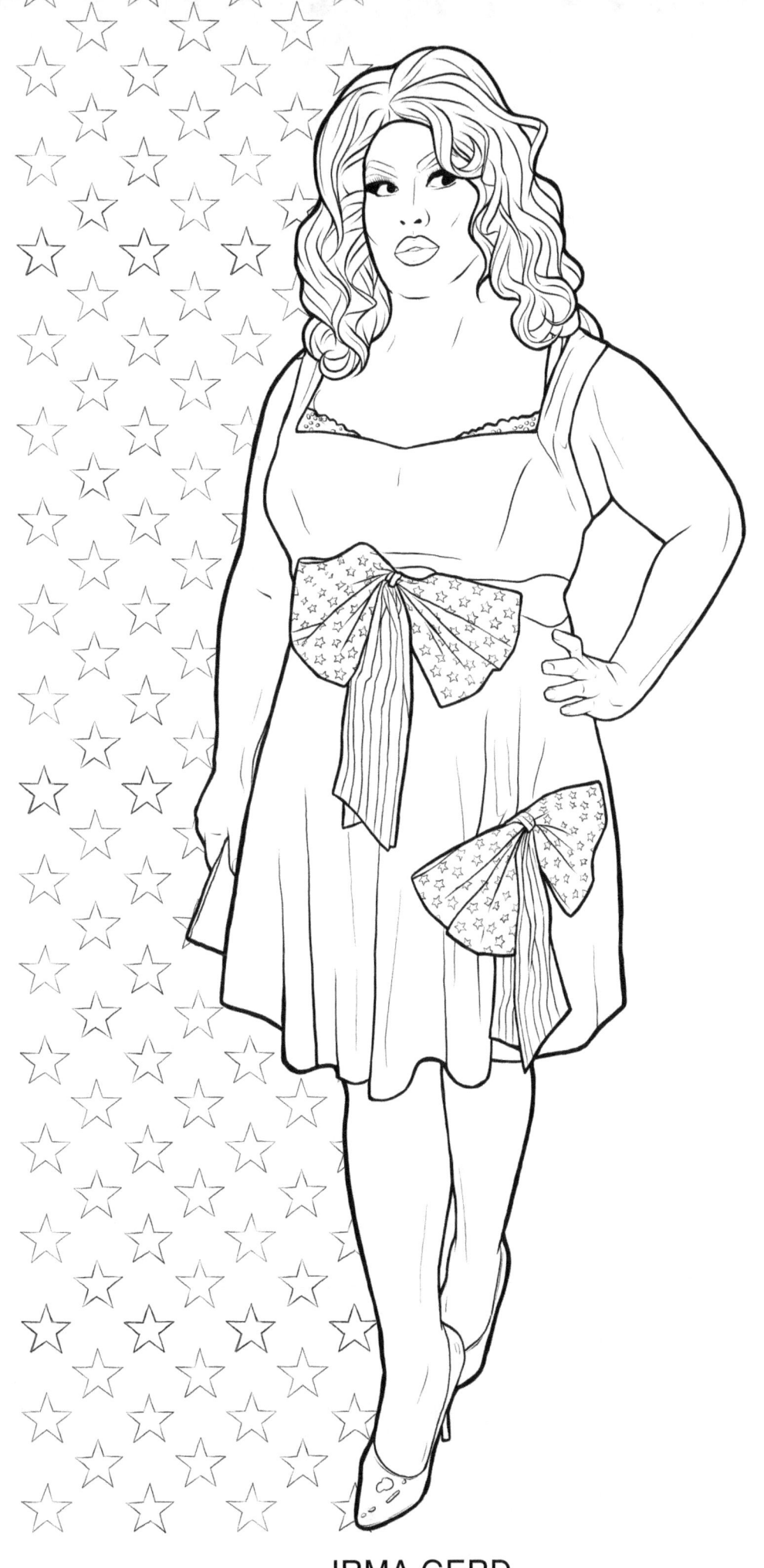

IRMA GERD

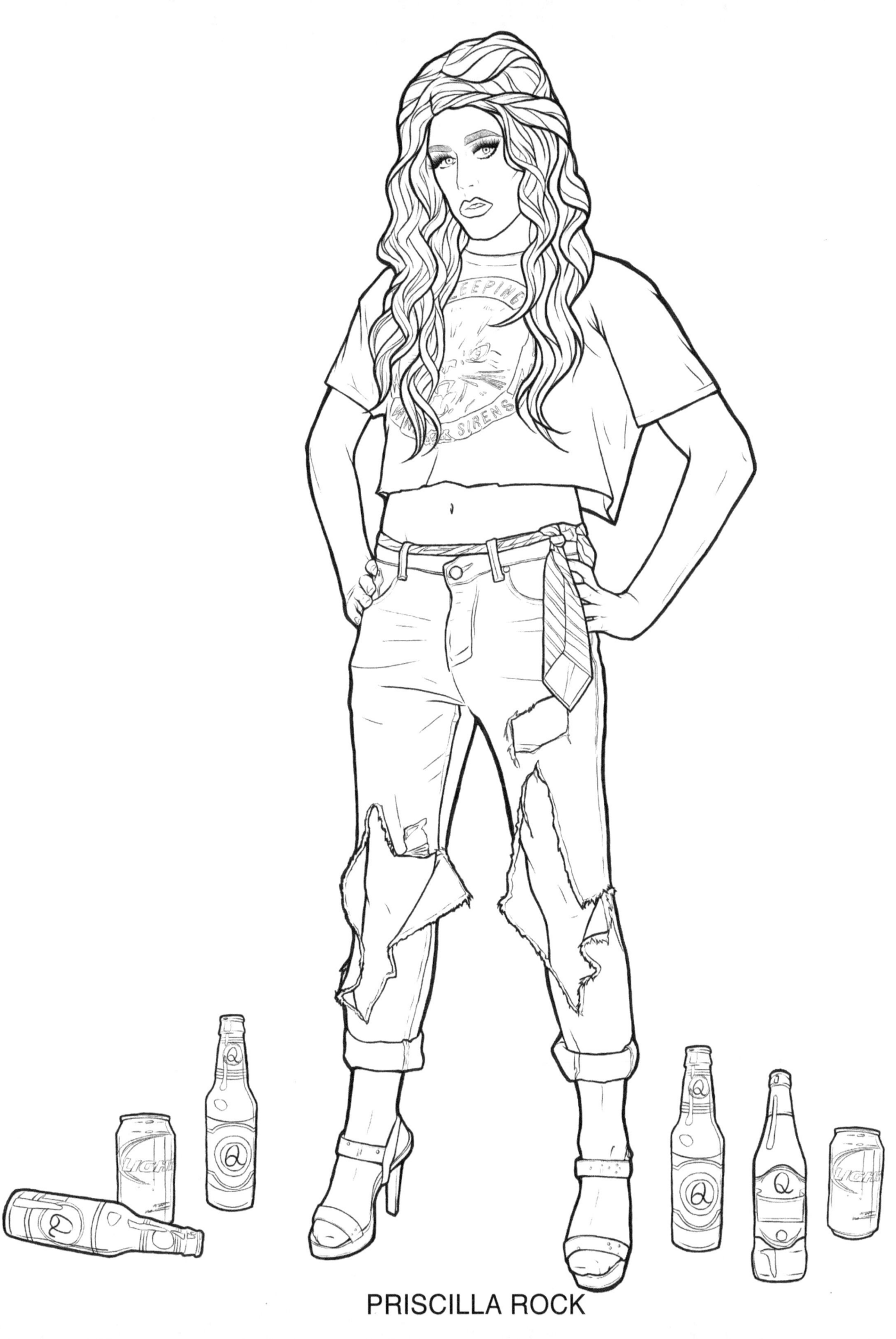

PRISCILLA ROCK

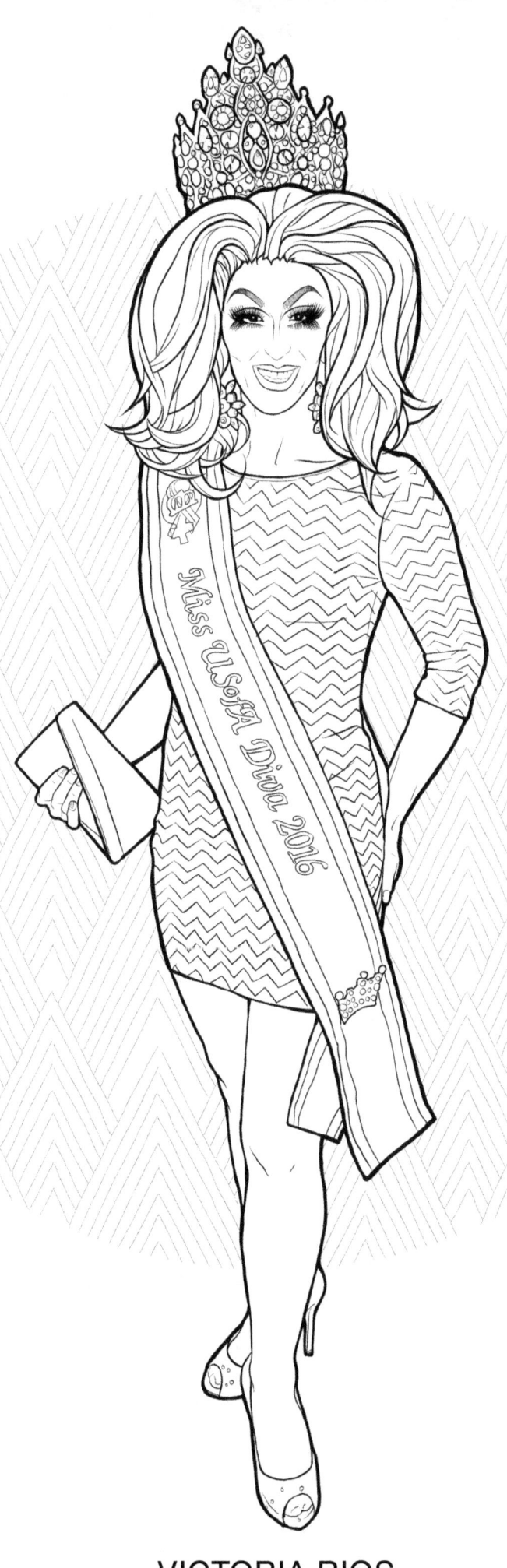

VICTORIA RIOS

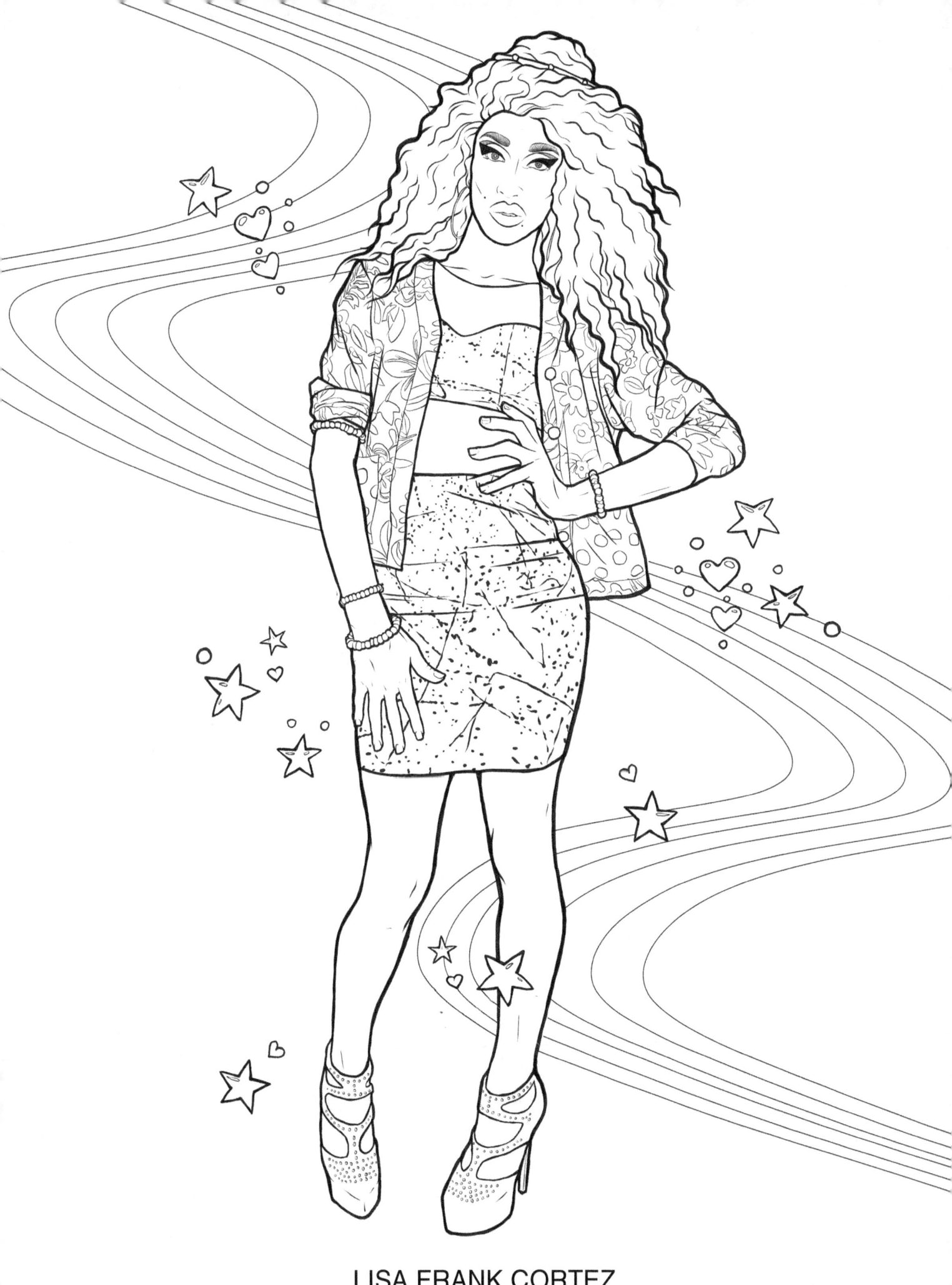

LISA FRANK CORTEZ

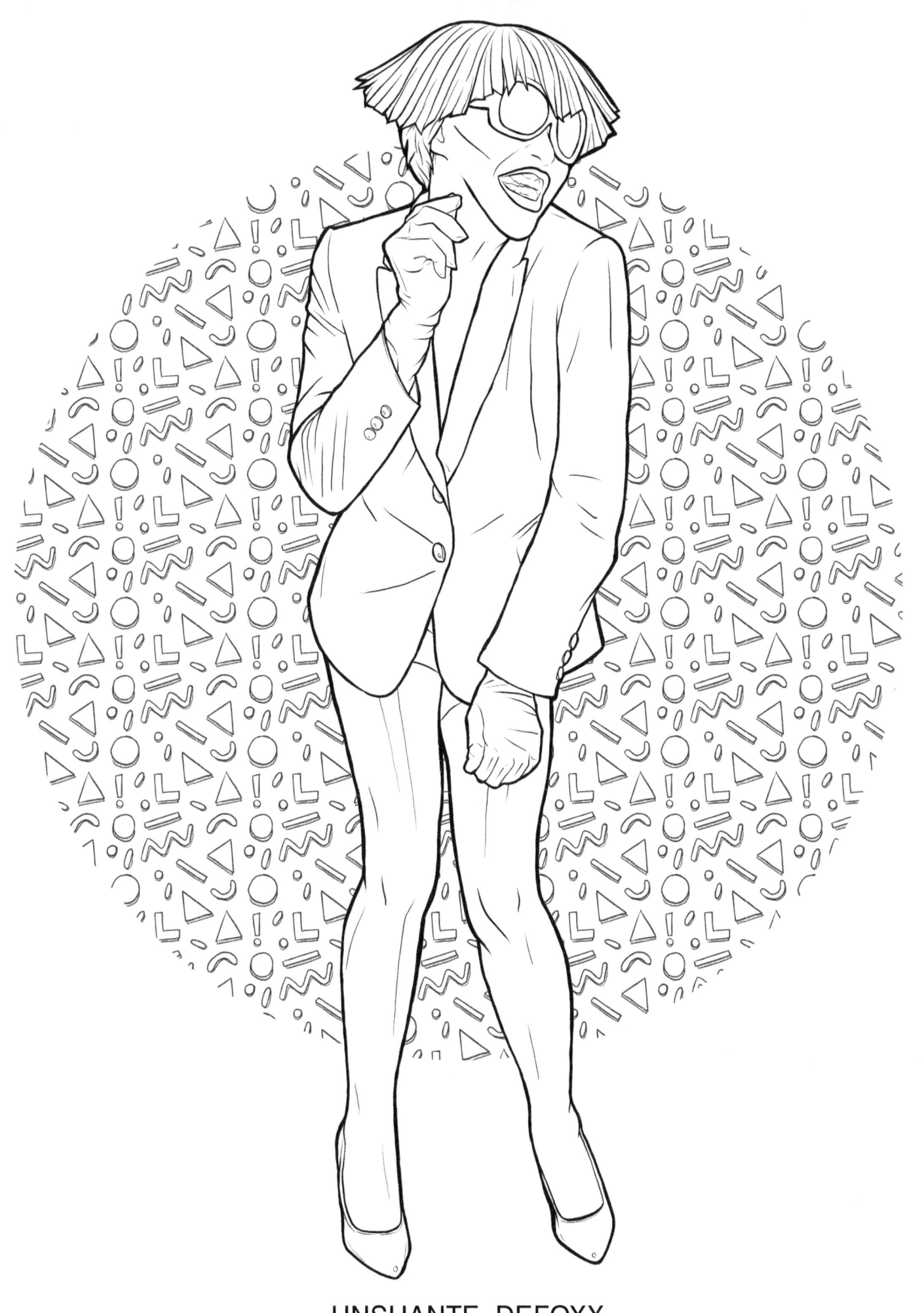

UNSHANTE DEFOXX

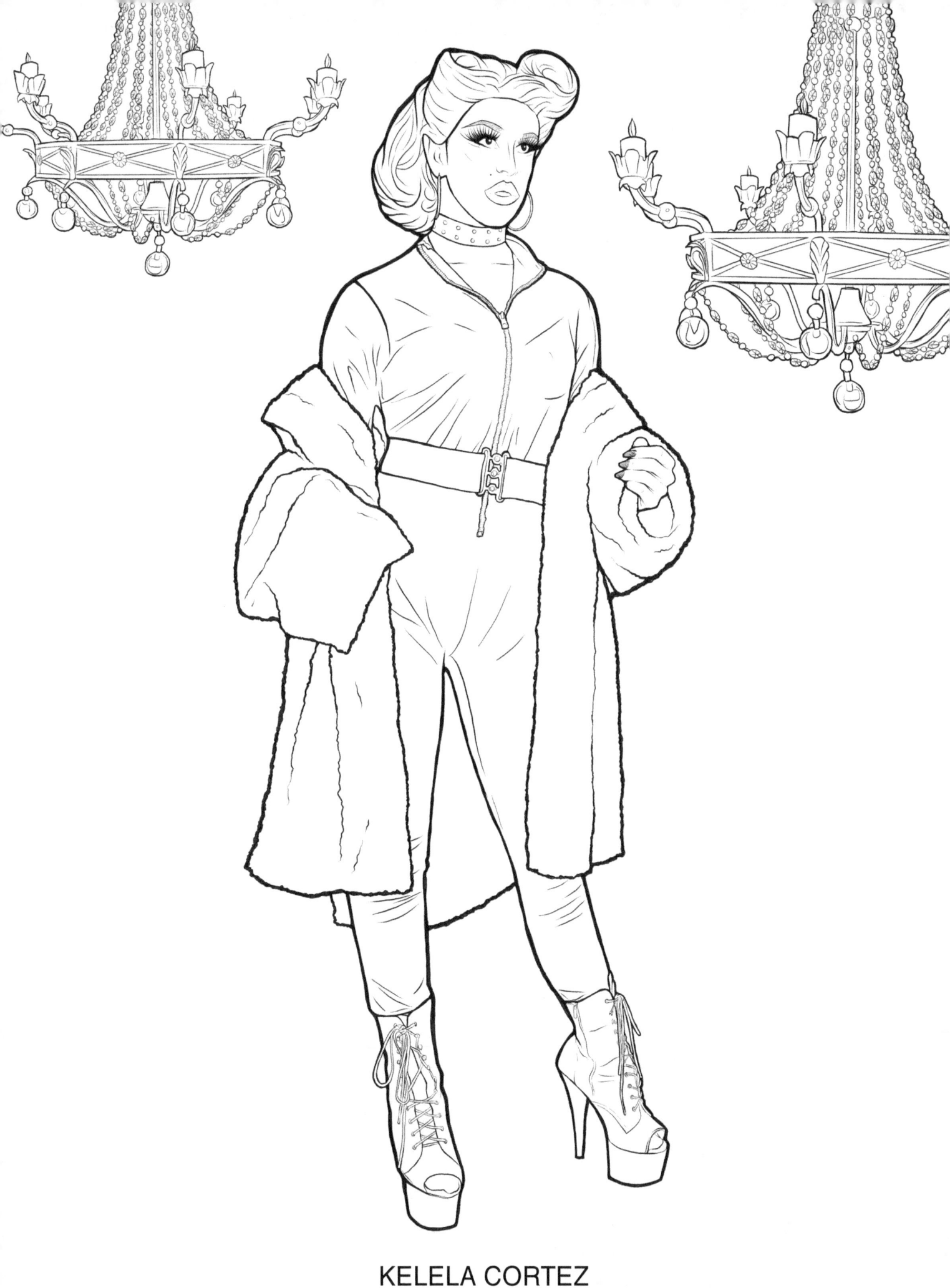

KELELA CORTEZ

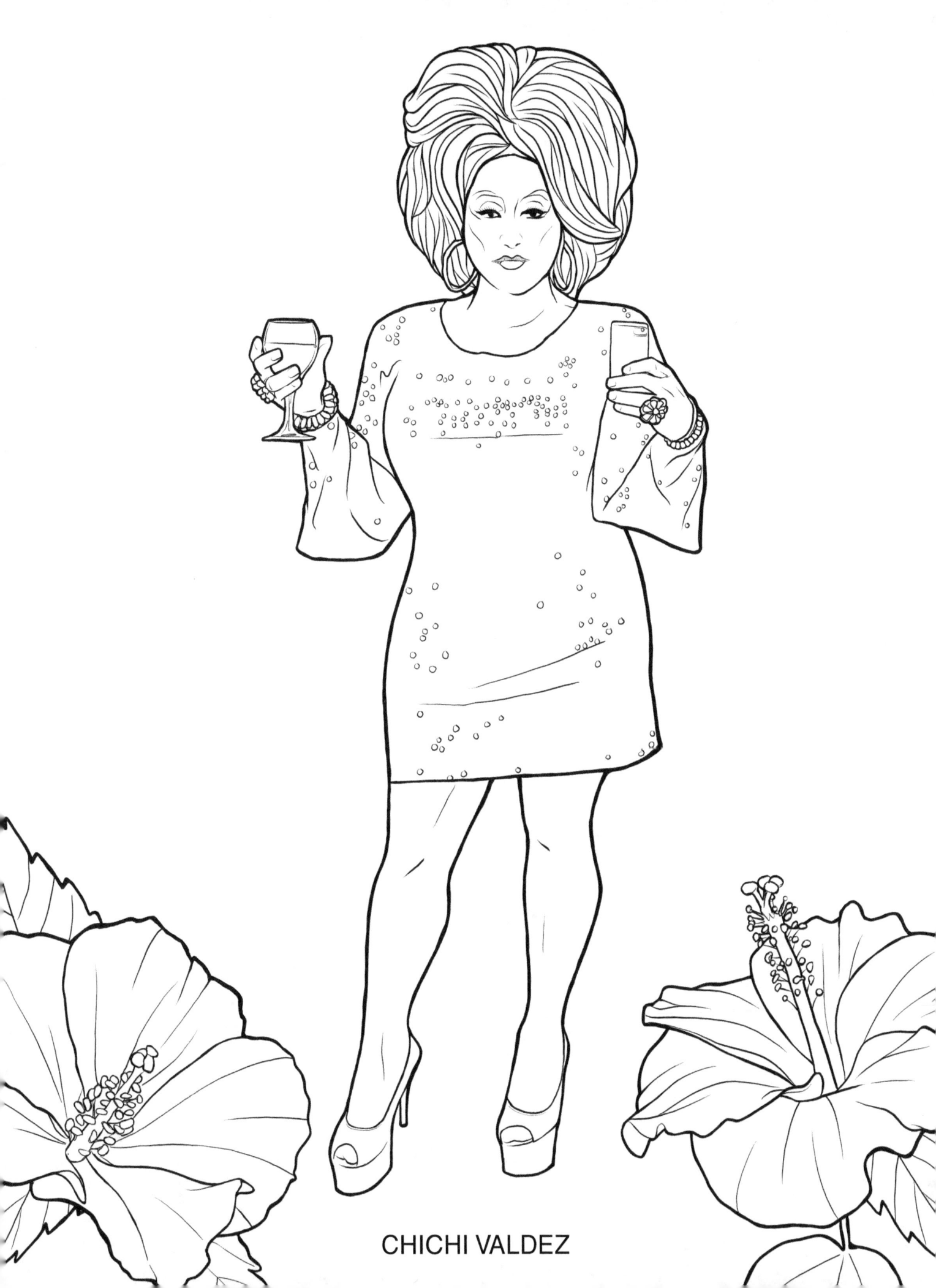

CHICHI VALDEZ

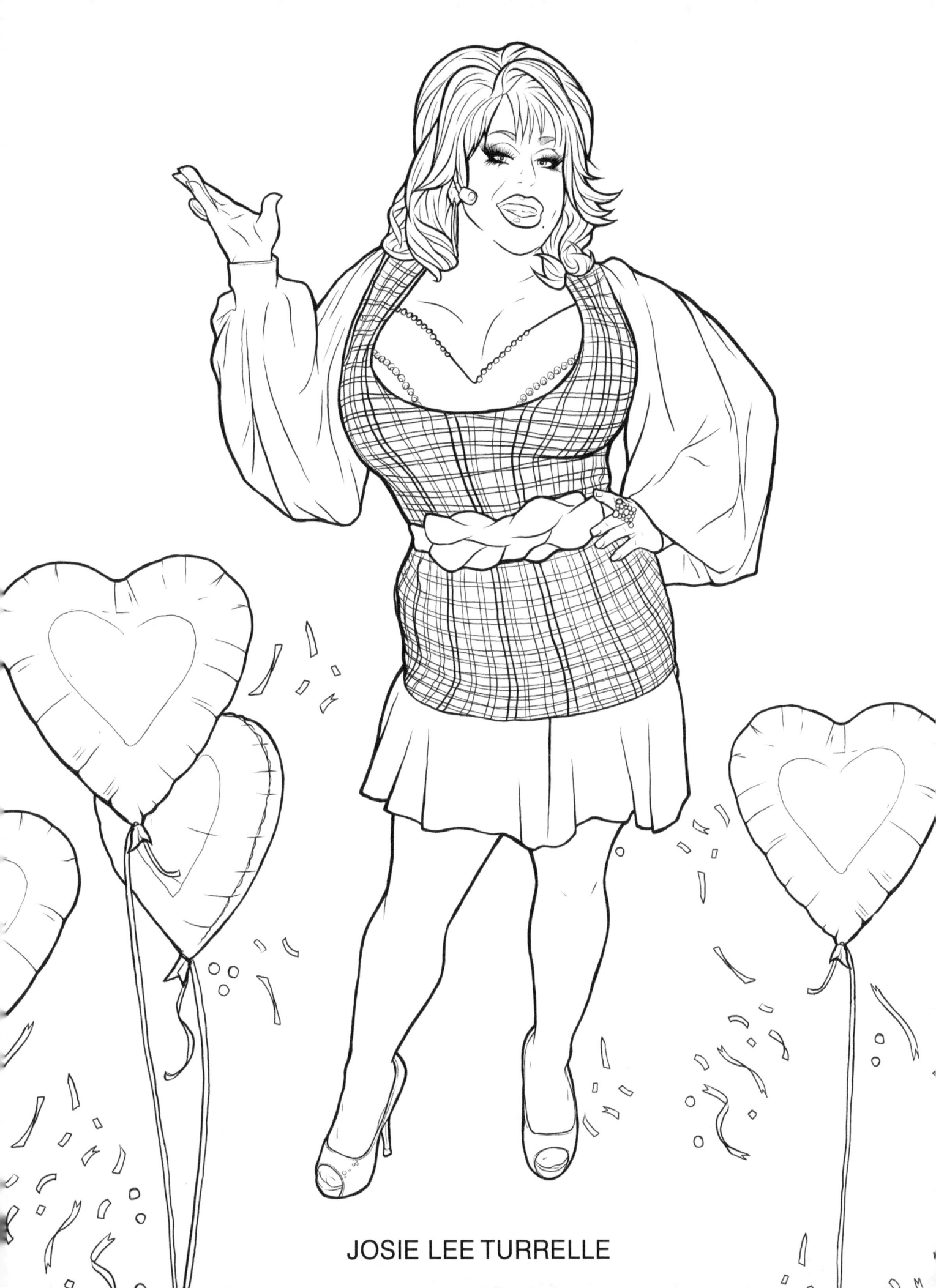

JOSIE LEE TURRELLE

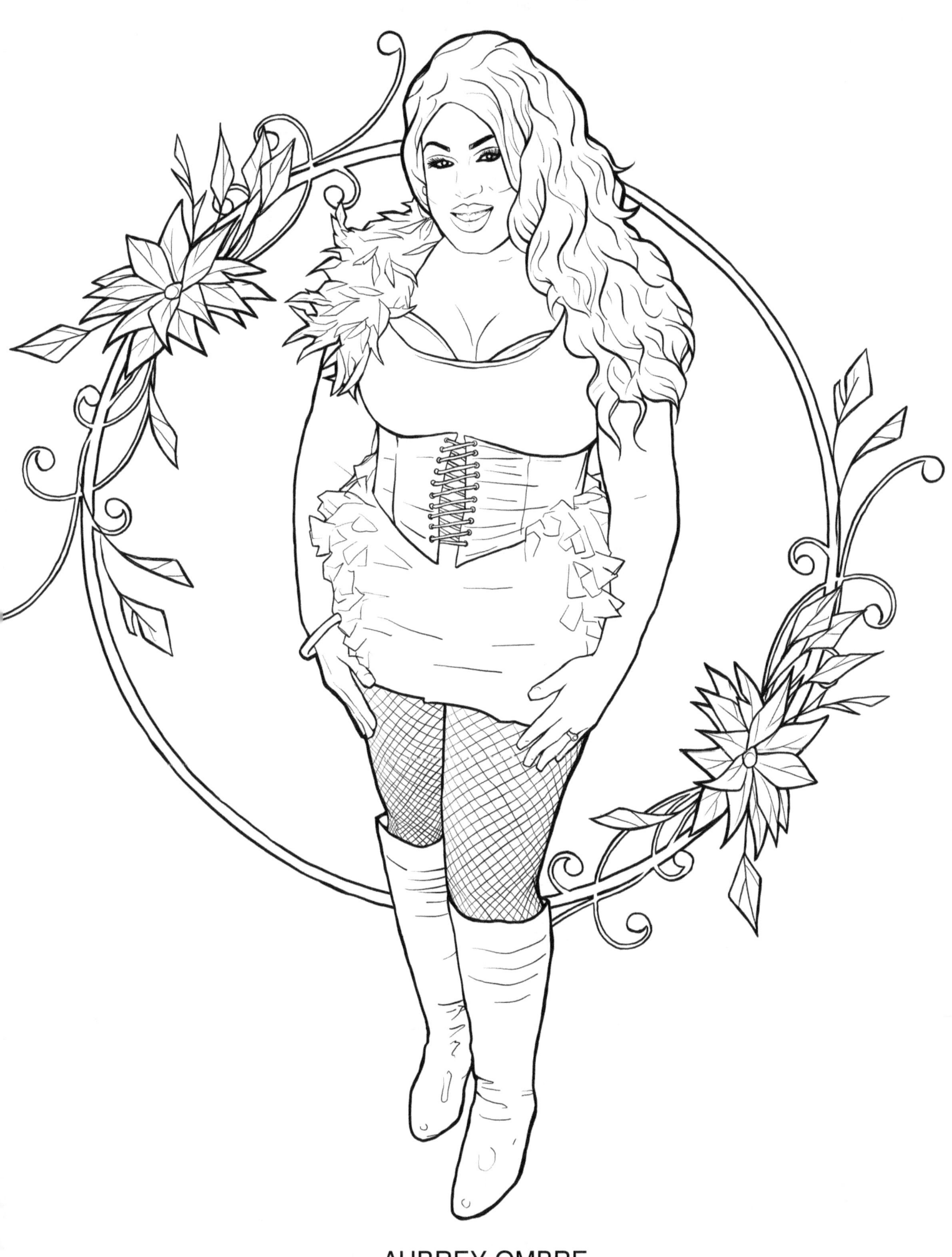

AUBREY OMBRE

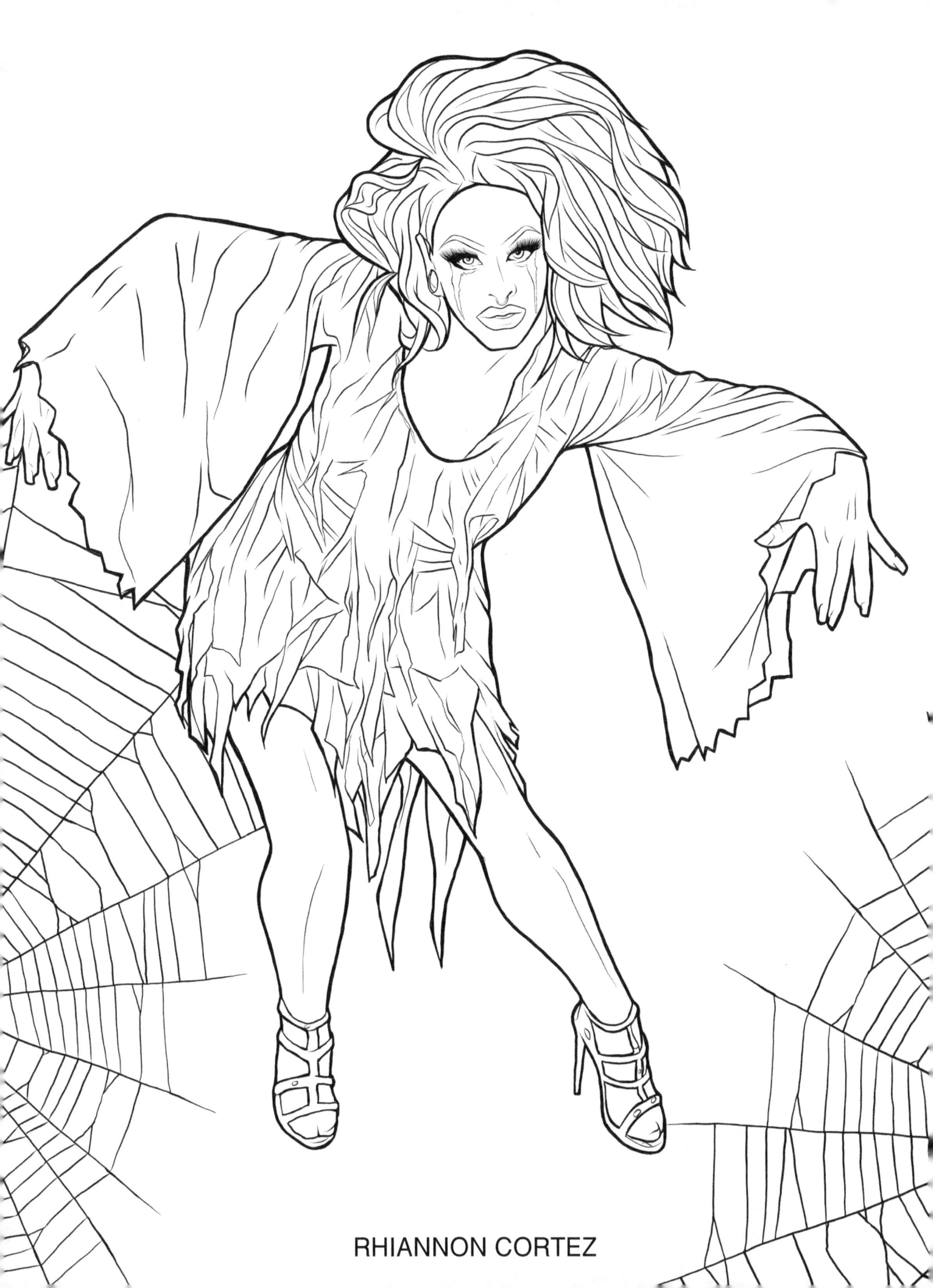

RHIANNON CORTEZ

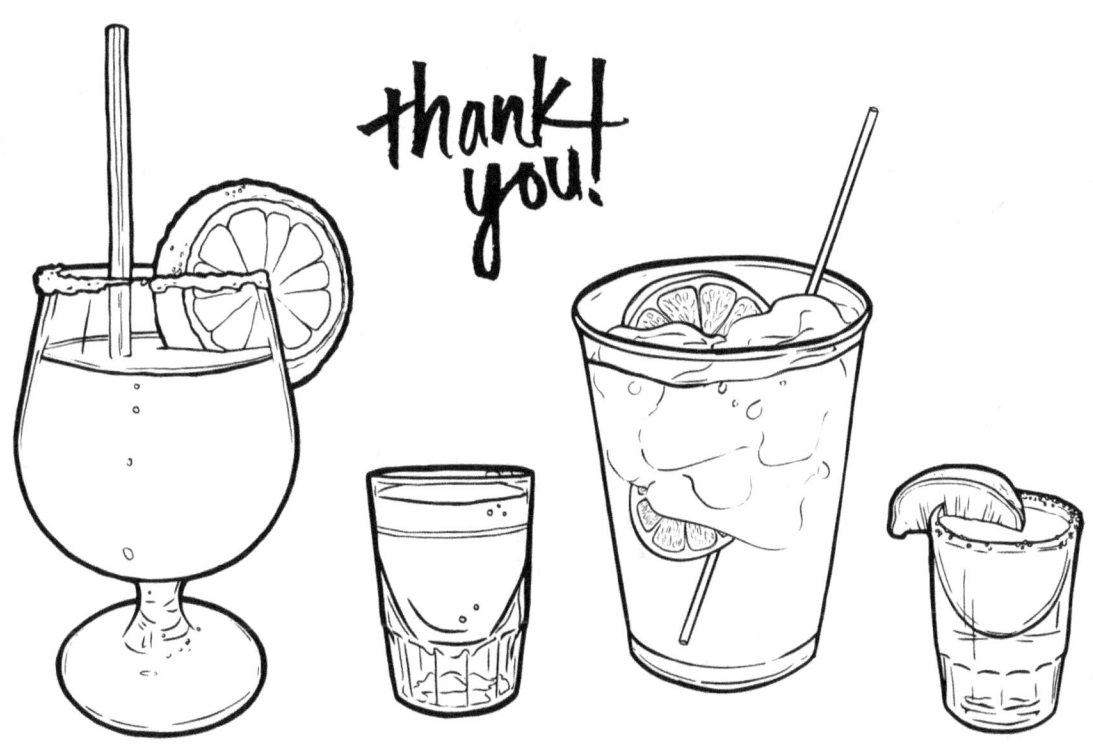

thank
you!

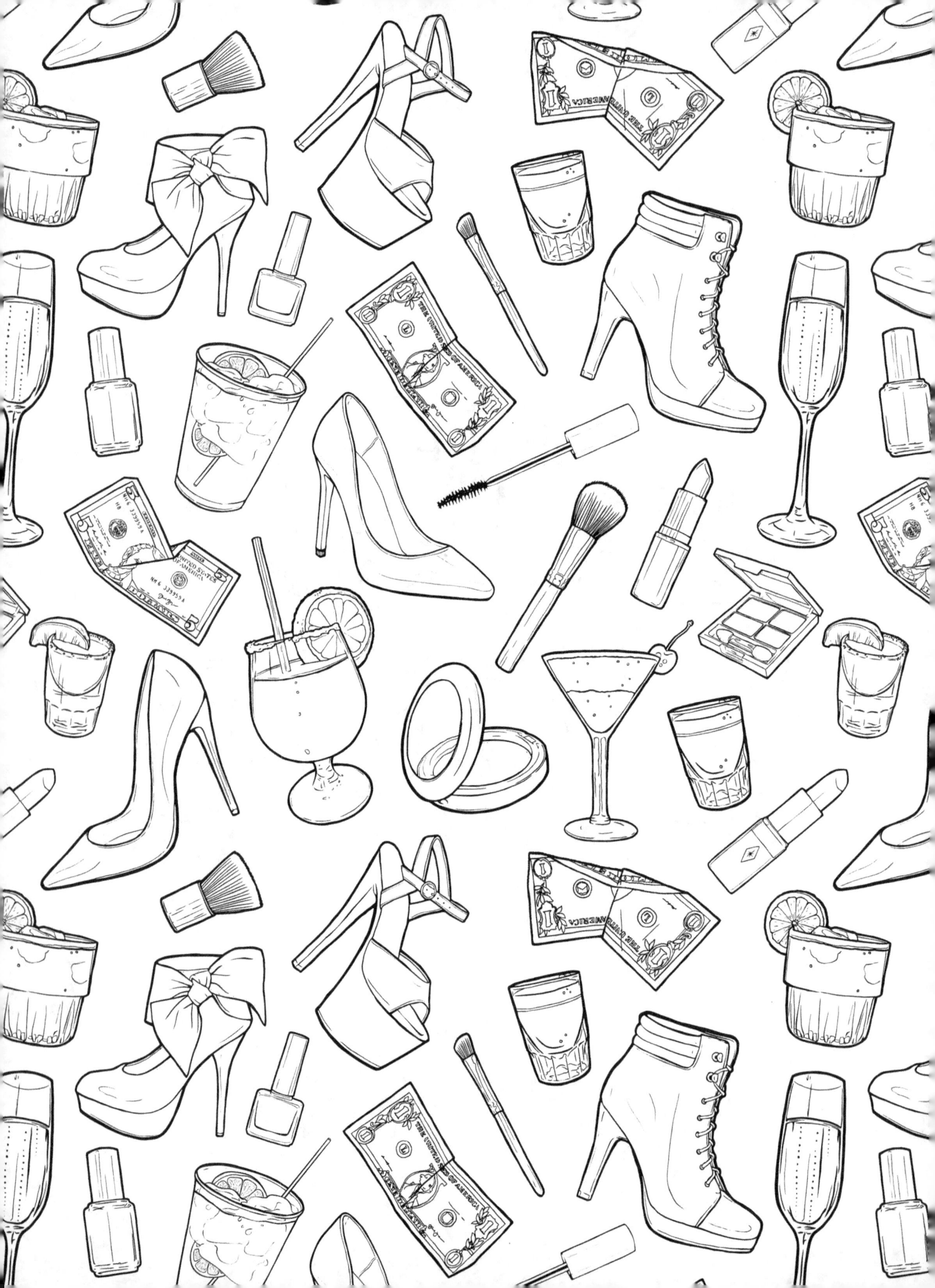

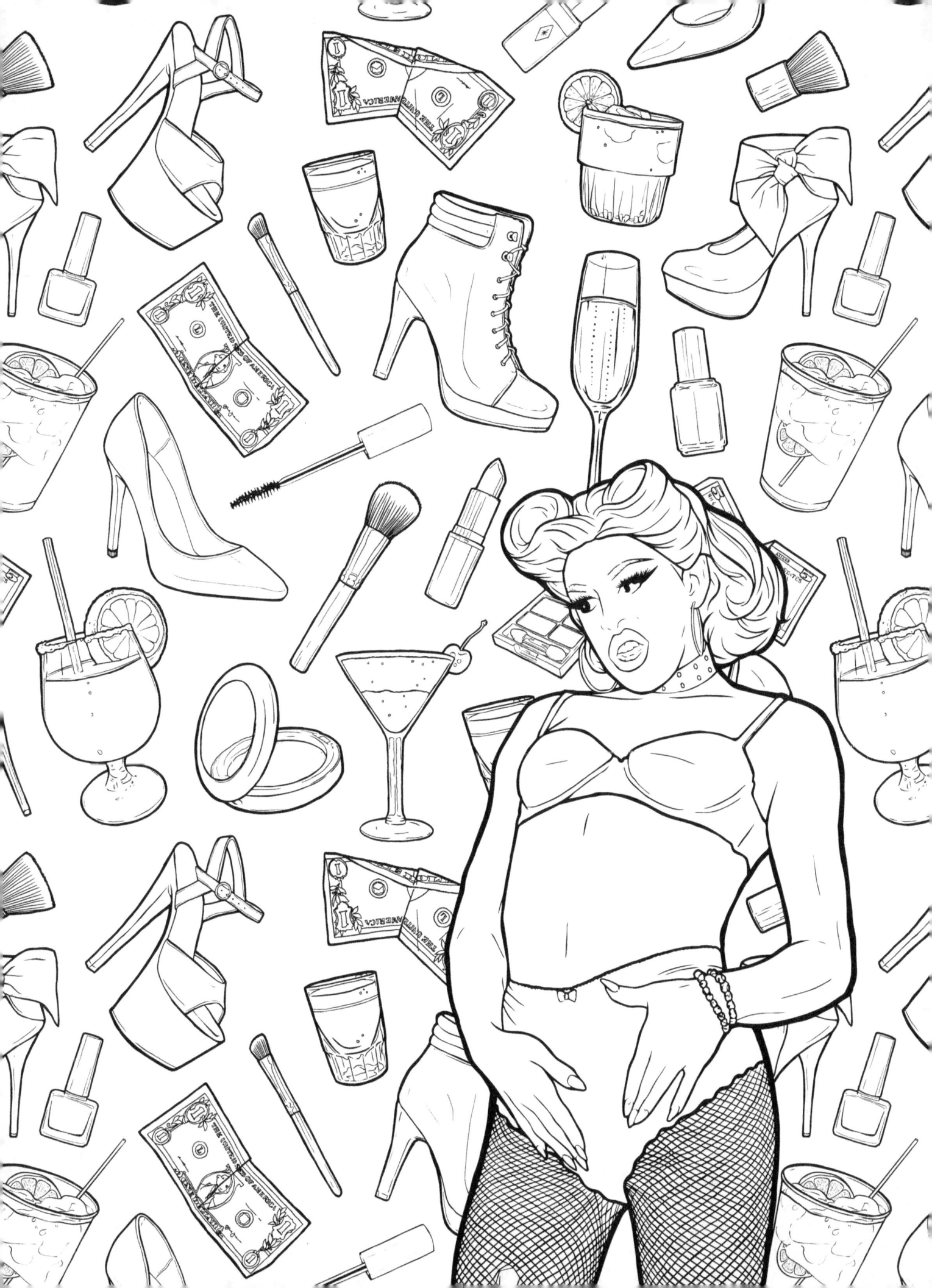